clouds

♡ love! ♡

poems 2020-25

larry goodell

©Larry Goodell
All Rights Reserved
978-0-915008-21-6

Poems for reading, for performing
in the free speech literary tradition.

credits

"Screws" drawing from *Peter Karassik: Drawings*, duende, 2024.
"Spittoonery" published in Unlikely Stories, Mark V - a tip of the hat
   to Ed Dorn in *Abhorrences*.
"Sand Verbena near Ojito Wilderness" and "It Seems" (here entitled
"Touching Spirit") published in *The Café Review*, Vol. 34, 2023.
"To the Dawn" in *The Anthropocene, The Covenant, and the Longest
   Night*, Placitas Solstice Publication, Presbyterian Church, 2023.
"Help Time" is dedicated to the Las Placitas Presbyterian Church -
   the *Earthcare Fellowship* and the annual Winter Solstice Poetry
   Ceremony.
"Equal Entry for All" is for Jill and in memory of Greg Johnston.

Drawings are from the poet's journals.

I acknowledge the full love and support for my life and work
from my wife Lenore and my son Joel - love has prevailed. lg

Cover created by Lenore Goodell.

duende press *(the original)*
placitas, new mexico usa
2025

clouds

poems 2020-2025

Free Free Free	0	Along	30
Screw Loose	1	Echo	31
Do-Nothings	2	Liar	32
What If	2	Hypocrite	32
Spittoonery	3	Connect Me	33
Sunbathing	3	End of Times	33
Book 101 Syllabus	4	L!e!a!d!e!r	34
Are People People?	5	For Jess Harper & Slim Sherman	34
Garden Retablo	6	Heard a Laugh?	35
Painting Lenore Goodell	6	White on Whites	35
Simple Life	7	Peter Karassik Laughing	36
Blow out	8	Courage at Naptime	38
Poet	9	Top of the Dung Heap	39
Purpose	10	Notes	39
One Single Man	11	Sun Moon	39
What I Did	11	Sentiments	40
Native Spirit	12	Protectors	41
The Pain	12	Mutual	41
Natives	13	The Indefinite Definite	41
Dawn Winter	13	Pointing it out	42
Arrest the Dawn	14	After the Last Game	42
Crazy	14	Routine	43
Diversity Wins	15	Miming Sappho	43
Boy Toy	16	Received	44
Crevice	17	Thunderbird Bar and Pool	45
Equal Entry for All	18	For Joanie - Singer	45
Deep Prayer	20	Thinking Thou Art	46
Are You? Are You?	21	Earthquake	47
Plight	21	The Space Between	48
Romancer	22	Lullaby	49
Octavision	23	Are You Prepared?	49
Nuts	24	Blue Space	51
Tongues of Babylon	24	Creator	51
What Can Be Saved?	25	Without Saying	51
The You in You	26	Earth Gifts	52
Equivalency	26	Yes!	52
Sand Verbena near Ojito	27	With the Flow	54
Touching Spirit	27	The First Junco	55
Mowed down by Reality	28	What Eyes	55
The Greats: Ginsburg and Lewis	29	Caught up	55
Quiet Speeds the Light	30	Mother One	56

Back to Nature................ 57	Relations.................... 88
To the Dawn - in Winter 58	T-I-T-U-S 89
Lovers...................... 59	Inevitability?................ 89
After the Great Ball Bust....... 60	Air......................... 90
Einsteinian Romance 61	Retribution from Fire 90
Super Modern Romance........ 61	Uselessness 90
On this Day November 16th 62	Diagnosis 91
Spirit Loss................... 64	Flyswatter................... 92
Brain Weather 64	Rad Way 92
No Ropes Attached 65	Song of Diversity............. 93
The Elements of Love 66	Generations 93
Timetable................... 66	The Obvious 94
Beautiful Nature 67	Evil 94
Empty for You 67	Impossibility of Escape........ 95
Fool........................ 68	"Even the Dogs".............. 96
Teachers.................... 69	Momentary Release into Now .. 96
Mousetrap - for Levi Romero... 70	Serpent Meditation........... 97
I Don't like You 71	Winter Solstice – Placitas...... 98
"Pootin" 72	Zelenskyy and Compatriots 99
Guns Galore 72	Source...................... 100
Carrier 73	For Lenore 102
Heart to Heart 73	I'm the Me I Want to Be 104
And Then There's Putin 74	Gloomy Gloom 105
Portrait of the Mirror 76	"My Religion Is Kindness" 106
Dark Opera 76	Celebrity Testes.............. 107
Trust Song 78	The Movement 107
Rain Run Raw Water.......... 78	End of Discussion 108
Mother of God 79	The Healing 109
Supreme Court Prohibits Sperm 79	Into the Mystery 110
"Have Mercy on My Soul"...... 80	1st of May................... 110
Dry Aphrodite 80	Why She Keeps Her Distance .. 111
Mind Rot 81	Heart 112
Content..................... 81	Advice to Myself 112
More than Once the Stars 82	Screams: West 4th Street....... 114
New Mexico Song 82	A Concept of the Pure......... 115
What Happened to the Sonnet . 83	Spring Sentiment............. 116
First Step 83	Ground Living 117
Fire Flood – Death of Oligarchs. 84	March of the Embryos 117
The Syringe Warts............ 84	Just Say Hello................ 118
The Trumpeta Line! 85	Fawn Fawn.................. 118
High Meadow 85	Some Sand Photographs....... 118
Seventies Brother 86	Old White Dude 119
Offhand Healing 86	Nature of Feelings 120
85+ 87	Developit!................... 122
Care........................ 88	A Lot to Tell Your Mother 122

29 Years	123
Did You Dilly Do?	121
Help Time	124
Heart Beat	127
No Joke	126
Dead Beat	127
Refreshing Work	127
Ba Ba	128
Homage to Char and Michaux	129
Crash Burn – *Give Us Singing!*	130
At Tingley Beach Preserve	132
Tasking	133
Rain Barrel	134
Portrait of Defeat	135
Cool Jazz	136
Look!	136
Looking at the Present	136
Dice Your Poetry	137
Man Made Moan	138
Made for Tv	139
Spring Water	141
On the Rise	142
Footprints	142
Golden Opportunity	144
Torn Sheet	145
Morning Glory	146
Spirit or Breath	149
Index	151

clouds

is dedicated to
Judy Grahn, Gino Sky
Kathy Kulp Hill, Ann Quin
and Ken Irby
like brothers
and sisters
to me
lg

clouds

pooems 2020-2025
larry goodell

Free free free off the charts out of hearts off the mind free at last, a new year to be free, a new life to be! Release of the devil's claw and free from the liar-ee! Free free free, free to breathe free to see, free to the stars the moon and night, free to the dawn free to get up to the day, free to be an American Revolution devotee, and so be free! Free from kings and cults, free from tyrants and their nepotistic buffoons. Free to be equal, happy to get up and be free.
Free free free!

SCREW LOOSE

There's a screw loose somewhere
      a haywire in the catastrophe department, 'cause
HE'S an *idol* before his worshiping mob
      facing and adoring his backside on public show
a crashing mix of lies and brutal entertainment.

      To not see this is simply to not see this –
a different set of eyes maybe, even a couple different species –
    actually the same species gone duplex nuts, double vision.

"I like the gross cinema, the taunts and piss humor –
   turn my Television Hero on or let him freely turn me on,"
     says one.

"This is a cord ripper from hell! Say goodbye to the Constitution –
   he plunges into the pit of violence and careless murder,"
     says another.

Too many human beings on this earth causes
   atrophy of common sense, it looks like –
too many scrambling for the bits and pieces of what's left.

   What's left?
Mother Nature, the Mother desecrated, the Nature –
   just to be fracked.

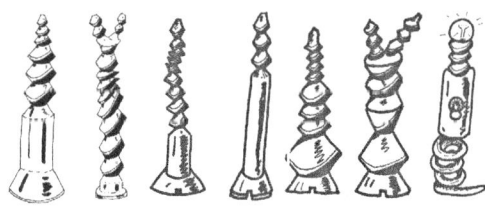

DO-NOTHINGS

"I will listen but I will not act.
I will listen and know, but not act.
I don't have to listen to know not to act.
The act of my act will remain secure.

No one can break my determination.
My act to not act is my only devotion.
I may listen and know – but I stick to my act.

I receive an award for my act of not acting.
We'll all get rewards if we don't act
and know or not know we do what we do
to get what we want going back to Adam
and Eve in the Garden and Jesus is coming
to bathe our feet and thanks for not acting.

The act of his coming and Father Above
who guides us to listen but not to act
do nothing about the wrong that is right,
the lying the truth, the fighting the fight.
To listen or not but never the act
of doing what's right which is never the way.
Let us pray! Do nothing today."

WHAT IF

What if the embryo of God were aborted?
    Where would we be?
Would we be alive in the mystery
    of what was and what is?

SPITTOONERY

Cockathoritarian
Liar*a*nucide
Heteroflattery
Chris*tem*orrhoid
Oli*ga*rgoyle
Diploma*sau*cy
Evan*geli*calisp
Trol*l*ocracy
Trumpoonery
Twatter
Celebra*tee*ny
Assholitarian
Bumperstickitooya
Abortio*no*poly
Cockamaniac
Prolifea*na*tics
Goonitude
Stu*pid*iturd
Republica*na*stic

Locker*talk*racy
Liber*pray*ian
Ty*ranti*kook
Plu*cock*racy
Melania*o*pia
Erikadonjare*dit*is
Ivankamononucleosis
Pharmacidal
Rapeogist
Gage*con*omy
Laissezfart
Authoricontrarian
Goosestepaholic
Petro*pen*icide
Ridiculitis
Billion*airi*cide
Trickledownocracy
Whitesu*prem*asick

SUNBATHING

Does the sky trade towels with the sun?
Can the sun go sunbathing?
Is everything naked in Nature?
Should all illogical statements be made logical?
Time will tell. What will time tell?
How can time tell?
What is the purpose of asking questions
about the purpose of asking questions?

BOOK 101 SYLLABUS

"I am offering a course in the 'book.'
What *is* a book –
something about its history –
when it started, when it lived, its death.
What is the difference between a book
    and a Facebook.
How much does it weigh or can it weigh?
Does it have a top and a bottom and sides.
Can it be opened or should it remain shut
and which side of the book should be approached first.
What can be in a book, what cannot be in a book.
  How long can a book last.
    Can the book harm you?
      Cautions to take when approaching a book
        for the first time.
    What *are* pages and of what importance
      do they have in a book.
  The process of turning a page in a book –
    step by step.
  What's on a page of a book or *can* be on it.
How to process the printed words in a book
and relate it to your phone viewing experience.
The value, if any, of a book.
Can a book crash and disappear?
Is there ever a need to reboot a book?
What to do if you encounter something troubling
    in a book.
What to do if the book expresses contrary thinking
    to your position on anything –
Book Therapy.

How to close a book and put it down.
The problem of what to do with a book once
you've finished the exhaustive process of reading it.
How to deal with the obnoxious persistence
    of the presence of a book.
What a bookshelf is and the proper way to place
    a book in a bookshelf.

Whether you should have a bookshelf if
    you have only one book.
Does having a bookshelf in your home bring down
    the value of your house?
How to conceal a book in your house.
How to get rid of a book.
How to cope with dreams of books.
Note: the next course will cover the essentials
in coming up with content that can *simulate* what's in a book."

ARE PEOPLE PEOPLE?

   Does the sky trade towels with the sun?
  Can the sun go sunbathing?
 Is everything naked in Nature?
Should all illogical statements be made logical?
Time will tell. What will time tell?
How can time tell?
What is the purpose of asking questions about asking
questions about the purpose of asking questions?
Can you continue through life being a child of 2
    when you're 82?
Is it terrible to be too familiar with things?
Everybody hold back, step back, just back off.
Let's all just step back from the precipice right before us.
  What is that gaping hole of tomorrow or is it today?
    People don't knit much, *or* play games, *or* tell stories –
      people don't seem to be people anymore.

GARDEN RETABLO

       This sky came once and then it came again
      in the garden high up over the Village,
     the green like no green I've ever seen
         that held the garden
   the garden of everything Spirit knows
   and the creature animal substances   locked in space –
twisting and wonderful coils in power
  with the red visage fanged with white staring eyes
   in the top layer over Earth –
   serpents holding green moons coming out of
         mouths of guarding beasts
   and dropping down, our Sun, our measure of all
    in that sky blue sky blue sky
      and the cherished below, our planet, our planet place

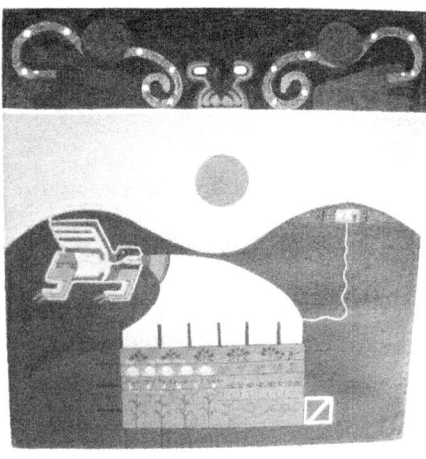

     the spectacular winged creature opening its entire self
    oh rainbow out our world. our particular made world –
   garden of lettuce broccoli corn tomatoes onions cabbage
   squash beets more of everything moves, and leading to it
   that little adobe house between two trees
   our dwelling as if it has itself grown out of earth
  out of the tree in earth, it itself coming from
 the air of the garden, oh simultaneity
of what's going on, our lives in the best
of the blessing of this painting from the wonderful woman
and wife who painted it out of our lives, its own life.

OH LOVE

Oh love let us be true to one another –
you know we do want more than anything
    to *love*
to overuse that word, to bring it into meaning
to find nothing better in the delicate
    fostering of relationships, I under use
that word, but now, in our sheltered condition
can't even go with friends out to explore
    nature's re-emergence, how the powerful few
have lost that word, "love" what is that when
you have to connive for more of the world's
    wealth. Wealth destroys love because it has to
    take from those poorer. Now I see myself
as along with others in our separateness.
To build the power of love if nothing else.
In my lack of organization I reach out
if only in writing, if only in being kind, kinder
    to who I am with and work here, while
the world seems falling down.

SIMPLE LIFE

Give me a pot with a little water
to boil my bone.
I'm happy with less than I own.
All I need is one or two molecules of air to breathe.
    I have a very humble chest.
        I sleep on two threads stretched between
            two match sticks.
                It doesn't take much for
                    a good night's sleep.
                        Just bring my wine portion
                            a couple gallons a day will do it
                            and I'll write a haiku for you
                            or a koan to pee on.

BLOW OUT

"What are we going to do when White Privilege
becomes White Non-Privilege?
What, oh what are we White Privilege-ey guys
buckaroos, buddies, good ole boys going to
we can't do that, do?
It's impossible and don't call my NRA
Nazi Religious Assholes –
    we're here to protect each other
ourselves, namely me. What am I going to do
if I can't aspire to becoming CEO -
Commanding Eternal Oligarchy?
White all the way, white here to stay.
Don't muddy the waters of my pristine cow's milk!
If I'm not first my bubble's burst.
Born to privilege, born to never thirst.
I don't get arrested when others are contested
bogged down in the courts while I
shop till I drop out of *fear* I've got to have
my unfair share, anything to block my
fear what it's coming to, *fear* what it's come to
as I come to *fear* what it came to –
    fear what it is!
We're not in charge any more it's THEM!
Shit! My front right tire just blew out."

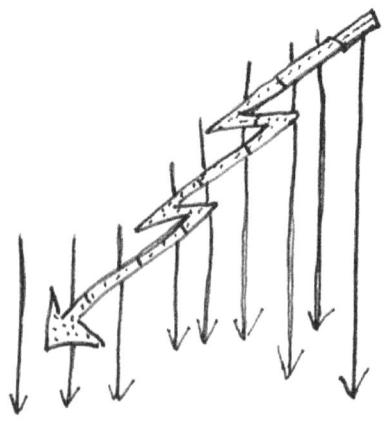

POET BILLIONAIRE

People may talk of love
but give 'em a few excessive bucks
and greed takes over the driver's seat.
It's so easy to justify destructive behavior.
I do it everyday with my   *(quiet)*
    mounting garbage container full of plastics
and some cans and too much trouble to recycle
bottles. As I think I'm doin' great
not using the truck that much and that's
what I use for *everything* essential.
              But
I have no assurance IF my poetry books
passed the million seller mark and then
many millions I wouldn't do everything
    in the books and out of the books
below and above the counter   *(louder)*
to reach the multimillion cash in
doing consulting for outrageous fees
and elephantine speakers fees as my   [elephanTEEN]
poetry phenomena push me up with
the billionaires and I'd figure out the best way
to get those books out for *less* and me
charge more and not worry about working conditions
of those below and assume they can figure out
their health care and all their needs because
you see, my friends have changed or rather
my tycoon competitor compatriots.
Hey, grab it while you can it's
the motivating force of homo sapiens.
But don't worry – poetry books don't sell.   *(quiet)*

PURPOSE

"The purpose of religion is to confer Godhead
 on lowly humans, make them feel special and blessed.
 A religion will do anything to perpetuate itself
  and to hell with anything that stands in its way
   including Nature.
 A religion is extremely selfish and doesn't like
  other religions.
 It wants to grow and be more powerful
  and blesses man and woman marriages
 so they can produce children to grow up and support
  the religion.
 A religion likes beautiful houses for itself
  and will not pay any taxes.
 A religion uses God as its Commander in Chief
to control its subjects and make them slaves to commands."

(in my opinion)
- *Zenkorkoff*✲2

ONE SINGLE MAN

One single man in power
dances on the tulips of destruction
tearing the flesh of the Constitution
the wild flowers of hope smashed
his history of a country cranked out of his ass
contrary to everything good, spits out bad
the death of a long standing tree of heart
every delicate flower turned into a button of death
why not push the rainbow of a sustained day
into a muddied toxic gray of sewage night
go backwards into some medieval torture chamber
and dredge up ghosts from tyrannical past
to trample on new sprouts of spring
prohibit growth rolling over every good tradition
turning back peaceful output of centuries of progress
of the flowering of first governmental compassion.
One single man and his humaneless false patriots
gives us the end of only the beginning
in the eyes of diseased toads
virus-laden bats of every horror
night sinking like black ink
into everyone's consciousness,
dancing on our flowering
the foundations of their
despotic mansions even
poisoning the ground.

WHAT I DID

I sat on a porpoise at noon.
He said what a lovely lagoon.
We played around most of the day
and I traded him in for a loon.

NATIVE SPIRIT

What is this God Thing that kept me up all night on
    a bed of nails? That racked my spirit with a medieval
stress till there was nothing left but the spirit to resist?
    It will not make me worship a Cube or Cross or Torah
no matter the torture since it is all in my mind.
    A mind thing a monkey thing an animal pacing a cage
a scurrying about that won't let me alone.
    Begone medieval trappings! You're an inherited plague
that came from abroad piece by piece person by person
    and struggled across this continent till I am where I am.
Rather, I listen to the place here and not its adornments,
    its transported, its transmitted, its trans-impositions.
The native plants, the seasons, the Earth presence –
    the gift of what is here, the returning hummingbirds and
absent juncos. The deer and the coyotes and everything under
    these stars, these stars. The breathing spirit down to Earth.

THE PAIN

      Hold me in your heart
  hold me in the part of your heart that creates healing.
      And let go as I deserve just so much.
Humility has to do with pain as well.
      There is just so much healing to go around
but I can share in that good part of your heart.
      And it lifts me through babying the pain out to
        cradling it and wanting it to go away.
      Go away in your very staying.
                Not so much accepting as knowing it.
As the healing, where is the healing setting in.
      The creative block of my heart opens, opens
  to the living reality of it, of me, of you our pain
        being overridden, entered blessed to be somewhat
           removed, again.

NATIVES
(incredible seed production)

+ + + + +

There are seeds of diversity
under every step you take
under concrete under a lake
where ducks paddle and glide.
Under buildings under where you stand
from seeds over millions of years
layers in earth changes.
And viable in earth crust
thrown out wafted eaten
and dropped to germinate
grow and flower
for bees and birds a living
diversity
right where we live
from fortunate water and sunlight
water and sunlight.
Look down admire foster protect,
don't step on
don't pick
let grow
learn from diversity
of native plants.

+ + + + + +

+ + +

DAWN WINTER

The common sense of *good* sense symphonically lifting,
    jazz beats the beats of heart,
      the ancient Hopi turtle shells, bells, skin drums becoming
      the heart of the planet, its Father Sun propelling
           transforming, coming back.
      Come back light light light, to equalize –
equality balance the never-ending end ended –
      vision sensation, lights and sparks –
light up inner light, the enlightenment of plants always somewhere
    on Earth.

ARREST THE DAWN

"Arrest the Dawn, charge it with Intrusion.
Charge it with Penetration of Darkness
for bringing a glimmer of hope *repeatedly.*
Charge it with persistent violation of the status quo
against all restrictions of change.
Arrest the Dawn for bringing any openness
to ANY revelation of forbidden truth.
Arrest Dawn with no judge no bail no jury no parole.
No reprieve. No appeal. *Lock it up* - for Eternity.
Drag Dawn's ass to the deepest, darkest, solitary cell
where we, at last, have enslaved Truth   for all time."

CRAZY, HEY?

The sacred subdues the profane or is it
the profane seduces the sacred?
Can you have one without the other –
the Satyr Play before the Greek tragedy
or is it the other way around.
It is so tragic you *must* have comic relief –
buffoonery, profanity, an ultimate spoof
or you might go crazy, in fact
you may *be* crazy and that joke
is your only key to sanity.

DIVERSITY WINS

Are you mad enough to be aware?
        Aware enough to be mad?
Does your insignificance
  in solving world problems
drive you crazy?
        Join the crowd.
We need to be loud.
     Our insignificance together
is power that stands up
to the Wealth Beast.
        Like the Israelis making change en masse
          restoring the judicial
  Like the Iranian women trying to.
Like the new Chinese to be.
  Like the new Russians to be.
     Like ourselves standing for peace
        and creativity
  facing the gun perverts
         with our Majority.
  Decocking the freaks of fake
  with art that won't let you go.
Hilarity penetrates falsehood
 and destroys it.
         It's time for a comeuppance
    of Common Sense
  and power of the Will of the People.
        And an evaluative direction towards
  a Planet half wild
and the other half, not sane.

BOY TOY

My phone
it is my bone
it is my tone
it is my home
finally the toy
has been created
to capitalize the world.
It's in your hand –
oh pardon me
for interrupting you.

CREVICE

        Sky powers of gonads
      should come crumbling down –
    those ever avant hammer feelers
  that beat their way into Earth crust
or indecent Babel towers stretching up
into the empty pockets and bloated bank accounts
of the rich and imperious, masters of impunity.
The reek of MUSK and the alarm noise
   of metasticized investments
      combine in bouquets of the dead poor
        as a chink appears.

        What is it, who caused it,
           it's there – do you see, now hear its
        widening, still small but fueled by
      Earth-demanded revenge that unfortunately
    and necessarily takes a few billion souls with it
  in one sweeping stroke –
deluge, burning heat, Earth opening shaking –
water swallowing phenomenon aggressing
   the unaddressed, the all and innocent
     who just wanted to gleefully cohabit
     and take more from the Earth. All –
        as the crevice shakes, appearing and appearing
     and appearing –
are pounded, affected, the virile maudlin gloated rich
and the innocent proliferating poor
   and the dumbfounded in the middle
     or what was the middle, no longer able
        to ignore its own militarist instincts
           and hypocritical self-righteous ego of
                its own uncooperative and torn species.

EQUAL ENTRY FOR ALL

God of the spoof boof reboot,
echo chambers all in line along the corridors
and equal entry in place
where you heard music as you
     passed along even greater wonders
Yodeling Operas and Cowboy Muses –
Native American Earth Heart Beating –
as it exists, it flourishes unhampered.
Comedians in a row, hilarious
     in a single voice
take care of you – Bach (to Beetles and Stones)
and a Schönberg laughs.
Is the chorus gay?
     They're doing South Pacific!

     Is it a palace or the imagination?
     Startling heartbeats compete with the Muse.
     Is reality true as it always was?

Suddenly there's a banquet and thank God
     you are not the speaker –
let somebody else eat their salad
     and find out it was their notes
          on green paper.
Shared thoughts of her LSD experience
     came to pass
but now everything is equal
     except the tired tyrants or would-be's
gnawing on filth –
the exhumation of their graft and greed.
So they don't live here along the ear canals
and twists and turns of the innards of Paradise.

Yes, Truth speaks out of ingenious evolutionary
    rewards of good minds
founded on compassion which was almost lost
in the mechanistic drones of massive destruction
killing maiming reducing to ancient rubble
    by the mean furious men of lost causes –
comedians in their blood that shout Death, jokingly.

    Here, the images of imagination are all real
    and again, there is a courtyard well maintained,
        comfort from the wind
    and seeds scattered almost everywhere
    around the rooms and of course the fields
        and along the roadways
    bathed by sunlight and moisture
        to sprout in the Spring.
    You can see everything from the
        open doorways and windows, can't you?

A museum of the ever-forming
where you did find dead spirits living along with the living
and that dinner arrangement, expressed with such care,
in the painting that no price can pay, given from the heart
as music is and was, as musicians could be and are
    the soul, the voice, the repair, the pause
the indulgence of real love, the inventive format refreshed,
echo chambers all in line, along the corridors,
and equal entry for all, as we sit
    down here
right here.   */for Jill and in memory of Greg Johnston*

THE ONLY CONSPIRACY IS THE CONSPIRACY TO ASSASSINATE THE EARTH

DEEP PRAYER

Mother of All
in fire and flame and force
    and fandango –
I love you.

ARE YOU? ARE YOU?

Are you an autocracy
    or a tall tree?
Which would you rather be?
Something for the Earth?
    Or dearth?

The question is opposites
opposites charming
or opposites clashing
    and harming.

A life of diversity
valuing a difference
or demanding a prize
for cutting others
    down to your size.

PLIGHT

                If violence isn't enough,
        what is?
        If you tear down what there is to tear down
    what more is there?
Tear down yourself?
If the country of guns won't stop you
    what will?
        Nothing. The will to injury and blame
            has taken over.
                Your fuse is shorter and anger
                    is on the tip of your tongue.

ROMANCER

Oh Romantic History of Know Nothing Land
with your curves and your curve balls and your Twilight Zone,
your fond history of Irma and Cavalcade of Stars.
Where is the delish dish of Nostalgia
    served on the toast of Oblivion?
        The dessert for the Last Supper that sends
            everyone to Heaven?
Has the constant persuasion to be something we aren't
    finally got to us –
        body mind soul and tacos?
Where is the mustard on the onions of our defeat?
Where is the Rainbow that falls down out of color?
Where is the finally getting everything together, alas?
The final tweak that joins all the pieces into one.
The compadre to the Big Bang that finally bursts into
    the front door?
The pharmaceutical miracle that combines every pill of
    Corporate America into a shiny dewdrop?
The Kiss that starts the beginning before the end of time?
Is it too late to drop off into the past of the future?
America, where is your stunning Maggot Pie or is it
    the Star Spangled Banana?
Moses' grandma who is not Grandma Moses sitting
    before the fire to tell you this –
Her trip to Mars or was it Vacuum Land where
    the turkeys don't gobble and the fish can't learn
        to swim?
What is the oldest story of all, now told to the
    newly married couple.
What is the Song of the Earth Spirits trying to rid themselves
    of pestilence that's blocking their organic flow?
Oh watch the late night show that has no commercials
    after the TV is turned off.

OCTAVISION

I got up with octavision –
suddenly I could see all over the place.
Miracles transform themselves into reality.
Time switches deeds for you and
    an avenue is spread out before you.
That's what I discovered this morning with
    the rain falling on the roof
and the memory of Mozart on the radio.

    Pull yourself into the target of home
    and await the dart that causes your fears to elope.

NUTS

Nuts in the to do section of Christ
    in the let go section of Buddha
        in the from-the-ground-up section
            of Native American.
                What can unwrangle the problem
        and clear the speech of craziness?
Letting all go and only doing
what comes up naturally from the Earth.

TONGUES OF BABYLON

            Can she see anything like floating tongues?
        Are visions acceptable in a nondescript world?
        Are fires pleasant if not too close?
    Is it tongues of flames or of real people?
Is *she* real? What do you see now strictly before you
and is it pleasant. How do you compare what you see
    with what pops into the mind. Or
does anything pop into your mind and you only see what you see.
    Are there any rooms to rent in the Tower of Babylon?
        Oh, Babel the Bible says.
        You better find a real room in a real house or building.
    Perhaps she is waiting there in that room.
She is sitting there having one vision after another.
    Oh Babylonia will we ever know *ya?*
        The time has come to sing a pleasant song.

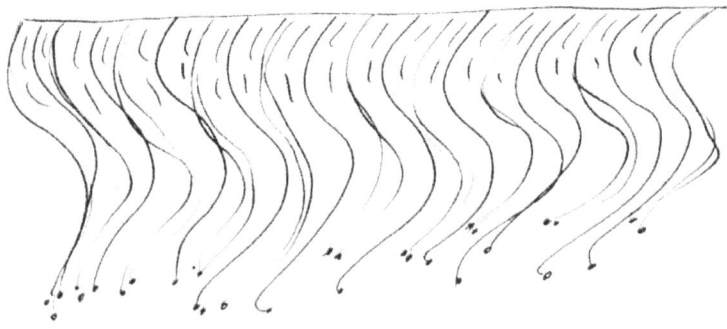

WHAT CAN BE SAVED?

       What can be said, what can be saved?
   The fabric torn beyond recognition.
What was it before, the flag of the United States of America?
I don't recognize the news except it be
from another planet, another space but not this one.
A time you would rather never existed, sadly
it exists. The stench of tyranny, tear gas
and total lack of hope, a backtrack into
a forward tragedy urged into motion into mayhem
by a singular amoral dolt of a man –
a beast walks on two legs and has no compassion
for anything, for anyone. This fitful beast
robbed convention of its use and tore everything apart.
And has removed our Country's heart and on it he feasts.

THE YOU IN YOU

The human race
has lost its face
clinging to every bit
of power
somebody else has.
It's not itself
but somebody else
it wants to be.
That superhuman
with the wealth
the glitter and shine
that's who
it wants to be
to be near
and contract
the disease further
of lost empathy
let alone
humility
let alone
sanity
"gimme gimme
I want to be
just like you
and walk in
your golden shoes."
Give thanks to
the appropriate one
your friend
within yourself
you thought had gone
away.
It-you-her-me
is always there.
The you
in you
the greater part
of me.

EQUIVALENCY

    The code of the equivalent
you and me
    the only thing that can take that
from us is inequality.
    Force upsets the scales
of liberty
    and power turns love to hate
if it intervenes.
    Allow us each to come together
peacefully.
    To talk things out
to come to
    a living consensus
leading to
    a common effort
to improve for all
    the best for one and one –
you and me.

SAND VERBENA NEAR OJITO WILDERNESS

Sweet flower of transformative light
as I get down on my knees bent hurting
to get my nose competing with bees to smell you
and stand, no need to kneel –
the aromas are wafting everywhere.

TOUCHING SPIRIT

How do I touch the spirit which is inviting me
    to touch it
as I reach out and it reaches through me
as if passing in the dark, in the light.

MOWED DOWN BY REALITY

Watch out when it seems like nothing can be said.
There's so much adversity, the world tipped over,
    the natural world depleted.
We are staring at our abundance
    and our migrant hopelessness –
Titanics everywhere on land and sea
as I watch the macho fantasy land
    of an old TV Western.
So this is what it's come to, *compadre?*
After you've shot the hell out of Nature
    killed the Indians and used up the water?
We'd better smarten up and put Earth first
    even though
it's too late and no where to go.
I'd go into that Saloon but I'd get mowed down
    by Reality.

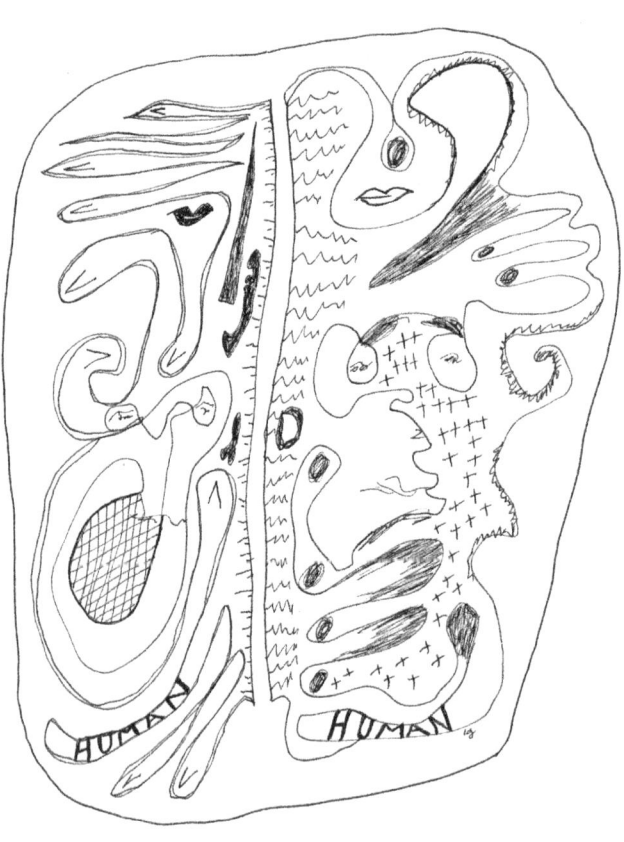

THE GREATS: RUTH BADER GINSBURG AND JOHN LEWIS

Without examples
so-called role models
the human being is lost,
subject to just about any
fad, swayed by any
celebrity,
even subject to a cult.
Becoming a worshiper
is easy as
eating a ham
sandwich,
a follower, it doesn't matter
who or what.
But then occasionally
someone of sterling
value comes along
through hard work
always
dedicated to the equality
of what is right –
the best, not the better
that a human can
do
and does it –
a life devoted to
all men and women
are created
equal –
and that person
is an example,
someone advocating
compassion,
the ideal that's hidden
in the messy
reality of life –
and she
or he
keeps value,
real value,
lasting hope,
alive
in the middle of
overwhelming tyranny
and greed –
the human's worst
proclivities.
She is who
I honor
and him –
rare beings
giving us
good and orderly
meaningful
and helpful
direction
to a messy
population
grasping at straws
overlooking those few
whose hearts
know no compromise.
Whole lives
can lift us into
what we could be
and do,
what we *can* be
and *do*.

QUIET SPEEDS THE LIGHT

Quiet speeds the light, as always
    and who am I here, in this atmosphere
to know it or anything else, but partially?
What brain could evolve to know a clear day
let alone the stars in infinite upheaval
    of the heavens?

LAZING ALONG

Don't trip and fall or
    find Oracles in your breakfast
or Soothsayers in your tomatoes you are growing
    or Wizards as you walk –
Idols in the garden carefully in the bushes.

You ride along on your stumbling
    elephant
with your mind on your mind
your body in your body
one half of you aware
    of the other half –
the wild animals in your mind
lazing along, unperturbed.

ECHO

How many wells will go dry waiting for a miracle to happen?
How many fruit trees will have to suffer from lack of water and flow?
Irrigation is *rain and snow*.
The water gods have not been appeased by care of Earth.
Human greed has won out in the war of dominance.
Nature, who has time on her hands, can suffer through
on one tiny planet in the universe. One tiny time.
Humility has been imprisoned and is to be executed.
All the dire warnings have come to pass in this tiny speck
    of a planet of an extraordinary cultural hope
dashed, as they say, dashed by cooperative ignorance.

Our little window here in New Mexico is but a glimpse
as we see the drying out, the huge volumes of automobiles and trucks
stacked homes and expansive ranchitas and dope-ridden domiciles,
villages layered in history tracing back to Spain and beyond –
diverse milieu in the stride of drought.
No matter where you look it's the picture of not enough,
as invasion of the Earth produces poison and need.
Thus a new year begins two thousand twenty, from
a Savior whose remembered message started out distorted
and was hacked over piecemeal for increasing power of factions
and God is used as an excuse to repress others by these lowly
warring humans. I have given up the ghost. I exist in a trace
of who I was, disappearing as my sense of things lessens.
Thin as my true place in things. Registering just an echo.

LIAR

The devastation of a liar lies not just within his soul
but the entire periphery that stinks, a tsunami of filth,
waves ever outward to infect others.
The turn of every phrase off truth enters like pox
in the pores of everyone around.
Finally the arrows of deceit enter the hearts of the slavish
and insurrection grows and grows, attempting to upset any
remaining vestige of truth. The solution is common sense, that is,
compassion and trust, that is, civility and open mindedness, that is,
a transparent and working democracy, the will of the majority.

HYPOCRITE

a hyperactive hypocrite
an idealized idiot
an ignominious ignoramus
a juvenile jackass
a klan-loving kleptocrat
a noxious knucklehead
a laborious lamebrain
a double-lying loser
a murderous manipulator
an amoral misogynist
a malevolent monster
a minuscule moron
a merciless muppet
a miserly muttonhead
a nasty narcissist
a Neanderthal nitwit
a non-entity nincompoop
a nickle-dime ninny
a notorious nit
a niggardly numbnuts
a no-goodnik numbskull
a pandering pendejo
a pea-brained pinhead
a putrid plonker
a puckered-lip Putinian
a calculative quack
a riotous racist
a rapacious racketeer
a resolute rapist
a showy shyster
a shit-dealing schmuck
a super-dooper simpleton
a seditious suck-ass
a shallow chauvinist
a swine-faced swindler
a treacherous toad
a two-timing traitor
a time-capsuled twerp
a treasonous trickster
a vituperative villain
a premiere white-supremacist
a yucky yacker
a yellow-bellied yahoo

CONNECT ME

Connect me with the spirits –
only they make sense with their lively mouths.
The sober spirits.
Nothing seems to come from anything any more.
It is all just what it is, with clamped mouths.
But in that hush after the breeze dies down
there's an electric spirit in the settling.
Now with the radio off I hear my heart beat
or feel it, it is like hearing.
I know the movement of a leaf on the clear creek water
 has no sound
while the creek is thundering this close over rocks.
It seems there is absolutely nothing in the quiet mind
 at 4:27 in the morning
except the eternal ringing in my ears
fortunately usually muted.
There's bound to be an element of the imagination
that takes true form but where is it
what is it, when is it.
Obviously it's in the stars and planets outside.

END OF TIMES

"Hello, this is the beginning of time.
The big bang hasn't happened yet
 but everybody is talking about it.
Since we're the beginning of time we're also
 the end of times
so there's growing anticipation,
a kind of extended nervousness,
a curious buzzing coming from all the nothing
 out there.
Oh, here it comes, here it comes!"
Bang.

L!E!A!D!E!R

A leader must have profound puffery of goose.
His head must be above all else as if his neck
was stilts.
When he walks, the Earth should shudder and
the stars start dripping jism.
He should be bloated larger than blimps so
everyone boy girl man woman maniac
can be afeared of bumping into him
for his hot air could explode in your face.

You don't want to get near a leader.
A leader who is a true bumptious leader
leads with stupid persistence, consistent ignorance,
superciliousness, a fishy presence of power
strength exuding from every bloated pore.

May his pomposity outweigh his soul
and he be the world's most endangered species
forcing everyone into his mold
of little tin men and some women
as he explodes into space and is replaced with
an extraordinary creative soul of a man or a woman
whose empathy and intellect of experience can
guide us back to Earth.

FOR JESS HARPER AND SLIM SHERMAN
(main characters in *Laramie*, TV Western Series)

The quality of your friendship will never be denied.
For those who would turn it into what it isn't
it transcends.
For where the accounting of it ended
it continues on.

HEARD A LAUGH?

> Heard a laugh lately?
> Skies are currently *gray*.
> But I laugh a lot.
> Sometimes at nothing.
> Or looking at myself in the mirror,
> that's funny.
> Screwing my face up even more.
> Jabbering made up words, real conversation
> in unknown languages, no language
> just jabber, but with real intent,
> passion or silliness.
> Sometimes a real belly laugh
> and it feels good.
> I wish I could tell jokes
> or could hear one.
> Let's hear it!
> Call me up sometime.
> It's windy and gray
> out there now.

WHITE ON WHITES

I'm sick of white puffery, white sugar, white flour,
white supremacy, white adultery, white adulteration,
white dominance, white dominoes –
I'm sick of white shitheads and black shitheads and brown
and *any* color shitheads, but here at home –
I'm sick of white ignorant assholes who don't give a fuck about
anyone else but their candy ass, white bigoted sexist racists,
white puffballs, white big business dickheads
white military tankheads, white cockamamies, white dominators
white power freaks, white dictators, any color dictators or wannabe
billionaire prickhead dictators, white militant survivalists,
white power nuts, white gas bags, white fatheads, white terrorists, any
terrorists, white conspiracy theorists, any conspiracy theorists,
white liars, *any* kind of liars, cheaters, thieves, white superiority nut
cases, white-washed whites, they're so white they're whited out!

PETER KARASSIK LAUGHING
Peter lived from 1944 to 2019.

A sky to cut to care to draw on
giant felled cottonwoods
he chainsaw carved
resting on each other in
isolated pieces across the campus
bold sky then, fresh youth
little carved pieces of wood hanging
over his bed
the dog would bite down, chew up –
so much for art, his dog, his art
tall and crazily sober –
Peter Karassik laughing at the
twist of everything
the sky couldn't be clearer!
It is all to be created, created again
writing on long scrolls of paper
an alphabet creating itself
forever scriggling to life
endless energy of Peter Karassik
cartoonish characters with
a life of his own, doing things
walking with a dog, alive dogs
never seen before creatures
funny minimal, sawing wood
looking in the mirror, shaving, with hat on
a life long series of panels of characters
the sky is not complaining but laughing
at the explosion of moment when
the blessing of two creativities
meet in one, carvings, drawings
spoons of chopsticks utensils portraits,
Mr. Sprout leading the way
as a large-eyed dog barks
or seems to, two color woodblock-like
splotches on paper like a recently
uncovered monk left us

quite funny revealed genius
creating through the world
like a tall skinny dancer
or an enlivener of your
responses at the wonder of its
seeming endlessness.
Peter Karassic so much more
than a mere poet can say.
The sky then lights up
with your gifts into now
the Tarot Holder leather
inside a stretched blue skin
over chicken wire creature
your hand outlined with
revolving seeds to grown plant
in the palm
your leather necklace with
dangling eucalyptus seeds
your ongoing crafting art into art
that a child could do if he was you
and we sat down for tea, on the floor
at my place as you introduced me to
my wife to be, a gift of a great eye
for art and creator too – Peter
as funny as it is, thank you
the sky is full of wind now
remembering.

COURAGE AT NAPTIME

"We're in a heaven all by ourselves"
said the Poet, wrapping his fingers on
the coffee table.
His new book lay precisely at a diagonal
on the table.
His partial lay doused with denture cleaner
in its plastic container in a closet over the toilet.
The title of his new book was
Courage at Naptime, Poems for Active Souls.
He let his jaw drop in a comfortable position
exposing his teeth gap
not caring that his mouth was open
since his wife wasn't in the room.
He starred vacantly at his chosen Heaven around him.
"What the heck am I going to write now"
he mused, "now that I've explored all those poems
about naptime."
He yawned wide and stared into space with his mouth open.
A fly suddenly flew into his mouth and out again
as the Poet stood up abruptly spilling his Earl Gray tea
all over his new book.
"I'll have to order more copies from
the Egomania Publishing House in Missouri."
The Poet cleaned up the mess on the coffee table
and dutifully closed his mouth as
his wife came into the room.
"The hummingbird feeder is empty, there's no suet for the birds,"
she scolded him.
"I'm in a hell all by myself," the Poet said,
begrudgingly mixing the sugar into the water
for the angry hummingbirds
and pulling the sticky suet out of its package
for the finches and squawking jays.

TOP OF THE DUNG HEAP

He lied before the liars who had lied about lying:
The truth nobody knows so everything you say is a lie.
To lie is to prevaricate, equivocate, fib
which is to accept falsification in the human species.
Everything that comes out of your mouth is the opposite –
what you need to do to get ahead, put your own personal stamp
on the cosmos. Delay, backtrack, confuse, depose, circumvent simply
go around always go around never attack anything directly
as a fact. Facts are the *stench* of reason. Avoid them.
Confuse your enemy with endless circular complications, sidetracks
perverse amusements, meaningless palaver, splitting hairs of
insignificance – till everything is a stall, *a giant stall* through which you
work behind the scenes to get what you want, what you want is what
you get, more and more to dominate in lying your way to the top.

NOTES

"Sleeping" in the physical realm of bliss –

(honesty is the best polish
and it shines on)

as your hidden physical pleasure
narrates itself.

SUN MOON

The brilliant sunlight flipped and became moonlight.
Out of the moon's two eyes was seen its transitory win.
The dark paradise flipped and sunlight washed everything
yellow white light. The bright day flipped and was night.
Can you see the moon? No, not now.
Just wait a minute.

SENTIMENTS

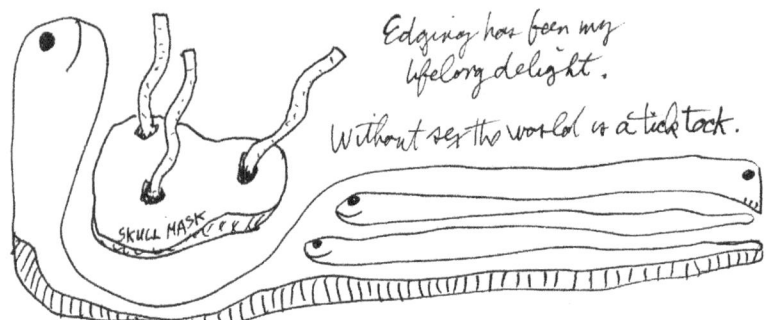

A race of infinite color
descended from the admixture of Americans
intermarrying over
so many years
producing a wild palette variation
in every family.

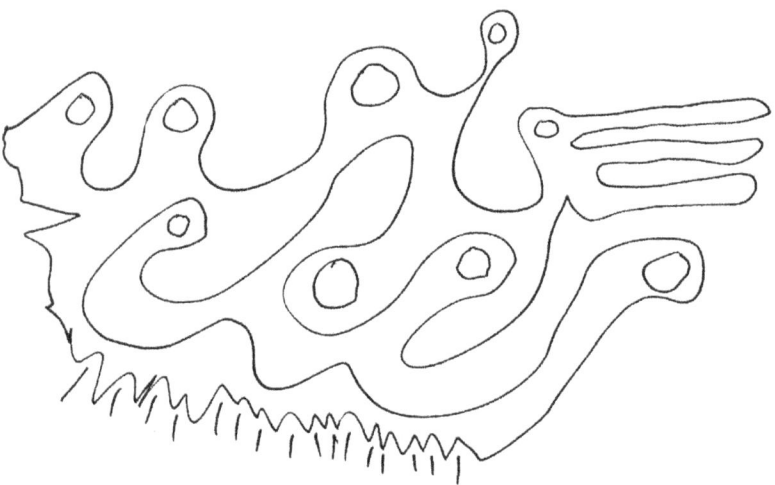

Poems come in many forms and fusions because
the imagination is never stagnant. If you're not attentive
you might be reading a newspaper column and thinking it's
a poem, or vice versa.

PROTECTORS

Insanity bubbles up to the Gods –
what are we going to do with this human failing
    that threatens to infect us all?
Well, Thor sends thunderbolts at it.
Aphrodite tries to love it to sanity.
Zeus is appalled and will have nothing to do with it.
Huitzilopotchli is attempting to burn its heart out.
Pautiwa darkens the sun in its presence hoping to lull it to sleep.
Souls of the Zen Mystics meditate beside it.
Thousands of Gods try various tactics.
    Nothing works.
Finally the insane bubbles dissipate on their own
    in the higher and lower regions
of the Goddesses and Gods and Earth Deities –
but Insanity continues in all the crazy elements of the humans
living dangerously and madly on precious Mother Earth.

MUTUAL

Waves of heaven, magical waves of peace intermingle
with politeness, willing to work, help out, do things good –
waves of relief intermingle with waves of Sobriety –
the opening up of life meaningful meaning full of life
partnerships meaning love, love meaning you and me
and him and her, love meaning us unspoiled, free.

THE INDEFINITE DEFINITE

Night in fine preference of sky
    burst of stars
the double open cluster in Perseus . . .

POINTING IT OUT

Here's my cat
here's my dog
here's the worm on my doorstep
here's my split hairs
here's my wedding picture
here's my Dad
here's all my sisters
here's my cockamamie Aunt
here's the debris on my phone
here's me as a baby or rather
here's a baby as me
here's the flush of insignificance
you've always wanted to see.

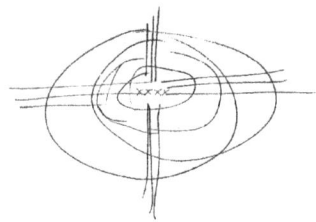

AFTER THE LAST GAME

After the football reaches the last dying hands
and there's nothing left but poof
who will think about the life that was?
The Earth finally unbeleagured,
will it start over again or rather
just be its usual transforming self
teeming with life and the spoils endlessly?
When the last race is run
the last baseball caught and dropped
the last weapon discharged in the game of war
will there be a natural peace, unheard
but self cleaning? A great relief? An overall
vomiting up of all the remains of humans?

ROUTINE

Borrow everything from somewhere
    and create nothing.
Throw up your hands when a new idea appears
    and say no.
Nothing refreshes anyway so why bother?
Why not look down the barrel of a gun, find
    your jumping off place.
Or rather, toss yourself in a well of turquoise,
feel the glistening of obsidian between your thumb
    and forefinger.
Admire an old pot you found half buried in the dirt
    on extreme North Rio Grande Blvd.
Stretch a nylon rainbow thread up from nail to nail
    for the morning glories to climb on.
There's nothing creative about any of this, this is
    routine.
Oh, you may ask, what is routine, about jumping
    into a well of turquoise?

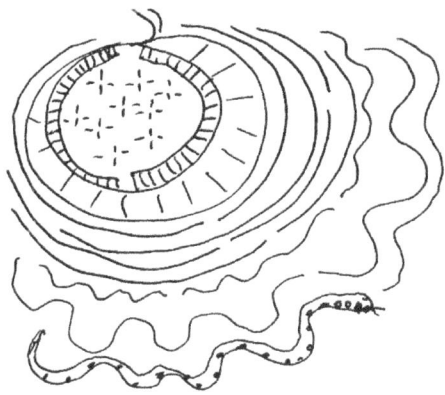

MIMING SAPPHO

The beauty of your body sitting next to me –
an avalanche so pure it   took   my   heart.

RECEIVED
(to whom it may concern)

   Thank you for opening an intergalactic voice
  a voice with no face and all mind. Creatures spoke
  all the way back to 3-sexed algae, interdependent
 on stars aching and stretching and waking up
as communications found origin on specks turned into planets.
   Although we haven't met,
I had tea with a commonly clothed Master
who gave his sex to me through generations.
The very image in imagination leaped from his hands
  rough as a man's, tender as a woman's,
hearing the declarations of articles of the Confederation of Freedom
the council of prior Gods with no distinction between
  the ancient Greeks and the modern Iroquois,
as voices were passed around during all night council –
the common humanity, the gift from the palm of stars, the fingers
  of planets
the limbs of constellations, the sweat of women
  working to free themselves from the oppression of men –
all colors of skin of the stars and planets
singing Equality whether listened to or not from obstinate fools –
  the vast empty space
of space of Empty, taking on power as
  the network holding everything together.
Thank you, lucky stars, who found companion planets formed
   from their motherly fire,
 the articulate lips and healthy hearty voices
 that make up the Mystery of Communication.
  That I be blessed by the Grace of your coherence
   is more than anyone can ask for
    and bit by bit receive.

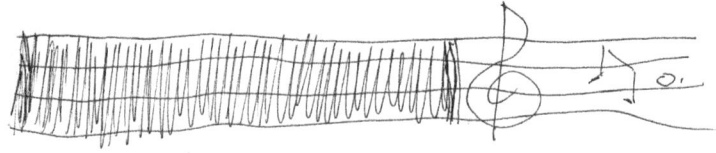

THUNDERBIRD BAR AND SPRING-FED POOL
for Bluejay and Ceil

Oh Rick, Bluejay, Fire Eater
holding your own in the concourse of the Bar
flames seeming to sear your unprotected mouth.

And Ceil, with the dreamy eyes that bypass time,
you wove me a sash. Thank you.

Lounging on the rocks by the spring-fed pool
Rick was beautiful, Ceil was beautiful.
He threw her in the pool.

FOR JOANIE - SINGER
(listening to her since the 70's)

Not to be missed!
Mot to be nissed!
Plot to insist!
Lots to persist!
Joanie Cere
what more could you ask!
History's story is still
a blast!

THINKING THOU ART

Be as slow as you think
if thinking Thou Art.
It's hard to put your finger on the button
    of activity or lack of
as all the organs of the brain are playing.
Play as Thou must in the Cathedral of Indifference
or let it ride without thinking.
Thanks and thinking have a similar root.
Thanks for thinking: that's a thought.
Think up Paradise. Are you in it? *That's* a thought.
Have license to think as Thou dost.
Dost Thou think at all? It dissipates the more you
    think on it.
Perhaps it's so slow it's just in the mind. Or was.
I've thrown thought against the ceiling before
    to see if it would stick, or did I throw it
        against the wall
or did I not throw it at all?

  The digital stream of my thoughts is hard to steady.
  Steady the course, meditate, but I've been *told*
  don't steady anything, just let 'er rip.
  I believe, I conceive, I consider, I deem
  I hold these truths to be unimaginable
  that all thoughts are created equal.
    Or in the vacuum of my knowhow, what little
        if anything I can know.
    Whatever it was, I thought it through.

Give thanks a thinking and a thanks
as slow as thou wilt, as fast as thou art.

EARTHQUAKE

Put good water in my electric pot to bring
    the miracle of the Earth to a near boil
and carefully pour on these picked and prepared
    green leaves
now faded a bit into perfection, releasing
    the essence of plants on Earth
        into my mouth my throat
            my loving pure body
        as old as it is
still alive to a little few things now
as I look out over my pale cup and find the center
    of my concentration carries me
out and back any place I'd like to go!
    Which is the inherent place I am.
Have you, too, been there before?
    Here again with you
the particles of the present all interrelating
    as we are all of us, every bit and precious aspect,
stunning together.

We might as well be on the cover of
    Heart and Mind Throb (the "Earthquake of Reality") –
hardly ever aware of, till suddenly the obvious
    breaks through.

THE SPACE BETWEEN

I love you - you are the space between my eyes,
    the jump from the Cosmos to Must Do,
the direction found at the pit of exhaustion,
the gap where my teeth were, on my lower gum –
all those years that have left my skin wrinkled.

It is the Now of Absence, the play of a string trio
    you've never heard before,
the direction of no direction, the press of release.
To be specific, the pause before trying to be specific,
    to put your finger on the passing question.
That urge, that popping up persistent urge
    to create this or possibly that
    or what is possible to be that.

Is it "I love you," that space between my ears
    between my two hands, my two feet walking?
    The movement of cell structure
    in the continuing bubble up?
That scream when the panic of your helplessness
    erupts, the relax of release, the "let go."
    The pause that becomes between two things.
The admiration for Sibelius a young Swedish student has.
The space between your thumb and your forefinger.
Thinking of the thought of things, it dissolves.

I opened a book and blindly pointed to a blank page,
    what does it say? It says stop what you're doing.
Do something else. Don't read too much into it.

LULLABY

Does anybody open stars as you do
pluck out of them fruits and vegetables
    as well as the lowly human being?
No, there is no twain, no twice born
only the open face of the Universe
    openly placed.
Unity is not a church. Dispersed unity is
arriving at the noise of a bull roarer
    sounding like thunder –
beyond human comprehension, or an ant's
    awareness.
Something cracked open comprehension –
    will the dawn come? Of course it will.
Stupid is as stupid does.
Faith is like a bed sheet, spread out in
    four directions.
Can you go to sleep now, with some comfort?

ARE YOU PREPARED?

The Moon wears a moo moo
    so where does that leave you?
The Sun is a strident figure, bold and outgoing,
    are you prepared for his turning up in two hours?
As the moon dances in its moo moo out of sight fading
    or dropping, dancing away below the horizon.

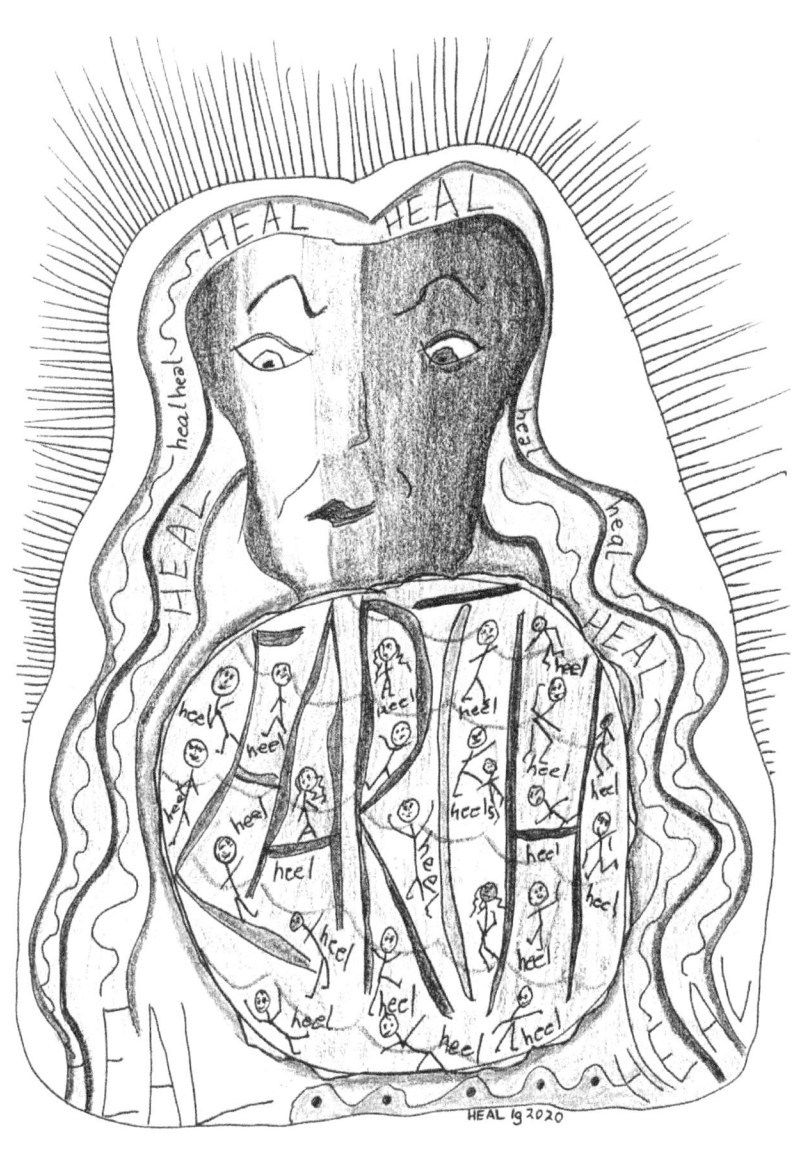

HEAL HEEL

BLUE SPACE

From the power of blue space, the healing
    Power of Buddha –
Moses lays his hands on the tablets –
Jesus is born of the seas of traveling Noah –
  her many hands surround her,
      Avalokiteshvara –
  his many hands,
    White Tara –
  her reaching the distressed,
      Green Tara –
  her mantra comforting the rest.

CREATOR

It is the Creator
if it is at all
and it is.

God is simply
an anthropomorphic attempt
to glorify
the human ego.

WITHOUT SAYING

Does love ever go beyond its definition
    to a time when it included all?
That is, it verged on the borders of God.
In fact, hey, what's the difference, I mean
love in its fullest definition goes without saying,
    gives in to it, is all anything needs –
is the source of other definitions, caressing.

EARTH GIFTS

Sweetest Coral, fire of time, open up the mind.
   What comes to you is lost before it is gained
      and a thousand young people can't be wrong
fighting for their future
   or is it millions and millions, billions
coming to raise the roof of dead leaders.
Obsidian, dark of the dead, now glimmering life,
Abalone traveled for, brought back reflecting
   light in rainbows.
Turquoise, mirror of Earth, come true
the values of what is present lead through
to Dirt guide, Silver surrounding youth hope.
   Out of transforming presentation
a movement of humility forever.

YES!

What is written is not wrote or rotten
or revealed before, stagnant *unless*
caught in midair as if capsized in flight
and captured to be revealed open to itself.
(But you gotta be quick, for that worded idea
is quick to disappear into that little black hole.)

Creativity explodes and is gone as the very essence
   of the Creative
is sure quickness, otherwise it would not be what it is.
So, that labored-tortured thing/idea, layored-and-fitfully
     produced
has expunged itself of all freshness, all connection with
  the Universe of Spark and Revelation and its swift opening
  to the Vast Beyond's yearning-to-be-heard, seen, *revealed*.
Oh yes, open open open to it what you're given to say –
  I say truly to you by being *silent and receptive*
     at the same time – Yes!

BALANCE

Nobody knows what the Shadow blows
that creeps over the instincts of men.
Men knowing the cold shoulder of their belief
will lead them to dominate as it wasn't
in the beginning – to rape was to take over
tearing down monuments to the female
part of it from beginning – to end.

    They became inflamed power, a population
of the trained tough, anthropomorphic gods
leading their trust in everything *but* the arts.
Listen to the *music* that transcends the past,
art that elevates the artist into the Earth
and brings back and carries on the Balance,
the Democracy of the Spirit that connects
long before the Universe existed and then
gave birth to Earths everywhere, each
separately coveted, blessed by its own diversity
as we so far apart from others like us –
must maintain in our female dwelling
our female past, our original bursting forth
from the womb we are only part, particles of –
the whirring insistence of all creatures –
we female and male humans just a portion.

    As music plays endlessly and art brings out
the balance again, the sweetness of liberation,
the health of listening, looking, creating out of
the Earth Gift Spirit. Arts are all hearing
seeing re-believed, feeling in compassion
the ultimate restorative thanks, that is humility.

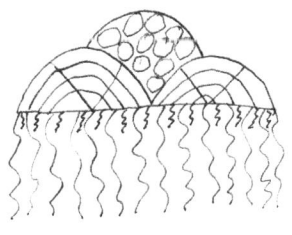

WITH THE FLOW

In the morning irrigating, water takes my
    thoughts with it
down the *acequia* to the garden to
    the apple trees.
My thoughts intermingle with water.
My mind carries my thoughts like water
    to you
Creator, hymnal singing of the Universe
Mother Goddess Earth of this Earth.
Water flows as I give you everything –
what good have I done with it
    what bad
        what mess?
If it's in your hands then I have a chance.
If I'm in your hands too: water force,
    water flow –
Creator of Universe I am too small to note
but direct me in anyway I need
    to be with the water going slow, slow
watering the garden, the garden of my mind too.
Take it all, take it, let it go.

THE FIRST JUNCO

The hummingbirds have gone farther South.
I kinda wished they'd take me with them - you know
where they're going there will be flowers –
but here, hello, the first junco.

WHAT EYES

for Wayne Jones (1939-2020)

Wayne what eyes what mud what arroyos what building
what maintenance what a voice what deep surety what
wildness what hollering what dancing what delight what crafts
what photography what images what reflection what music
what darkness what light what pecs what strength what
celebrations what wars what protests what compassion what help
what madness what peace what history what memory what family
what life what lives what living, what peacefully wild being,
what friendship, what astounding mutual respect, what honoring,
    what peace.

CAUGHT UP

    Stars are after me
    Heavens join the chase
    I run like a dog but
    the Cosmos surrounds
    and puts me in my place!

MOTHER ONE

　　Mother of Creator
　　　　from whom all blessings flow
　　the Mystery of your First Form within us
　　guiding each of us, flora, fauna as they say –
　　solids and creative space
　　the growth patterns, the death patterns,
　　the exhaustive urge to understand
　　the given simplicity of the in and out breath,
　　the air and the bees
　　　　all plants
　　and animals including ourselves –
　　you in your manifestations
　　　　exclude all manifestos,
　　include inclusion as
　　　　your be-all and end-all.
　　Bring healing to our dear ones, to ourselves suffering
　　as we honor the gift of our Planet from the Created Creator
　　　　brought forth,
　　the beauty of all things living in harmony –
　　may we protect and bless and preserve and mend
　　　　as you are the healing and the health
　　of all things in Nature.

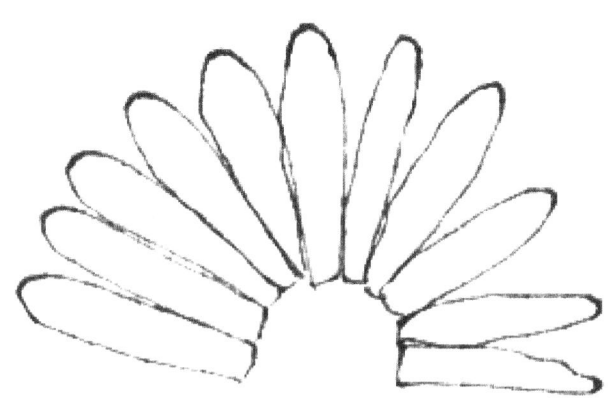

If all the said is said it seems so sad.
Words fall off a rock
and into a pool, what pool?
The pool of insignificance.

BACK TO NATURE

As God dissolved into Love
love became the only hope
of a tortured planet,
that is
love for the Planet.

TO THE DAWN - IN WINTER

The light that scatters dreams came to me and said
"I am propulsion too, as moving it all along creates things
and what's hidden blares out with motivating darkness –
a thousand violins scraping on gut strings as the
    movement succeeds – fingers striking the taut metal strings
        of the guitars too
      the whole orchestra of light   lifting the darkness
        which is better, *light or dark?*

✳

You tell me, lost in the dark, stumbling around, or, give me the light
    even when it penetrates, burning the soil and drying up the water.
Give me the light, it will move it all out – antagonistic politics, finagling
    greed, selfish negativity, throats sore from its shouting division –
move it out, dark dealings
    the black *straps* of ignorance and delusion
        strangling from sheer over-numbered, multiplying menace
    of *one* species –

✳

the human in its darkest hour manipulating its genes so the wealthiest
    can absorb and control, bending an entire race under control,
        feudal times
updated fearlessly, algorithms drumming at the door of light
        to tear it down –
as the built up propulsion   builds up scattering nightmares,
    the common sense of *good* sense symphonically lifting,
        jazz beats the beats of heart,
            the ancient Hopi turtle shells, bells, skin drums becoming
                the heart of the planet, its Father Sun propelling
                transforming, coming back.
            Come back light light light, to equalize –

✳

equality balance the never-ending end ended –
        vision sensation, lights and sparks –
light up inner light, the enlightenment of plants always somewhere
    on Earth

✳

the *breathing* not the last, but the first, infiltrating Peace and making it
    whole again –
dance of electron power, *that warmth* in partner with *that cold,*
    that dark,
ever in spiral centered dance giving the erect human species
    one more chance before Nature's *Solving* Takeover
        lighting the Truth even brighter.
✳
Take humble leader of the Earth Mother or, or, or, follow down
    dark mass graves, rather. Don't you think it's the dawn?
        Dancing – in that heart music."

LOVERS

I never wanted to get married but she hooked me
    with her sky hook
and pulled me into her chamber behind Cloud Nine.

The kiss that exploded on Mars
pulled me in with it in spite of the atmosphere.

It was that kiss on Earth, on Earth.

AFTER THE GREAT BALL BUST

Organic Fairy Dust,
two-toned Elves
shelved for the future
but you know they're coming back
along with the Gremlins
- baked or unbaked -
the half-baked Giants and Shmoos
and dewdrops of Sprites scattered
and forming a Rainbow in the air –
the hobbling Hobgoblins
reappearing at some time, some time
after a colossal time to come when
rhymes disappear,
Gnomes Goblins and Imps
in the Spider Web future
leaping legless Leprechauns
along with their musical neighbors –
Nymphs, Pixies and Mermaids
appearing again at the seashore
along with debris
from the cargoes
of rusted out old ships
capsized during the World
Ignorance Debacle,
the Great Testicular Explosion
we all know is coming,
the Great Ball Bust
that destroys imagination
along with the dwarf Genies
and tip-toeing Trolls.

Don't worry, they
and more
singing their particle songs
will come back, as Earth
dear Earth is their partner.

EINSTEINIAN ROMANCE

The Spirit of the energy of time
collapses space
as unknowns surpass knowns –
you guess what is true and guess what?
It's true.
Did you forget what that Black Hole
      said to you?
   As you sped by?
"Don't say goodby, don't say goodbye."
The biggest suckass of all time
craves company.

Einstein's gigantic mirror image
needs congratulating.
At 16 he opened the key to the key to the key
as he sped along looking at the future
which is heretofore known as the past.
"Echo universe, I'm with you."

Is it an echo of the big bang, or *duh!*
the Big Bang itself.
All questions are answered between the lines
and that fuzzy old genius is perpetually smiling.

SUPER MODERN ROMANCE

They didn't fit together
though he was a she and she was a he
but they were unparalleled
in love.

ON THIS DAY NOVEMBER 16TH

Mother of my Night
the love that comes from you
and then from you - what is its capacity?

>Your source and source's source
>always going back in the mind
>beyond the mind, mine is not mine –
>giving birth to the birth all the time
>quietens down in the dark, dark hand
>cool – and yet loving
>as I am now, the benefactor
>of quiet and a pen and notebook
>and Mozart's Piano Concerto #18 in B-flat Major
>coming through the CCRadio by my bed –

the creativity of ordinary expression
on this day to dawn on which
November 16th 1532
Conquistador Francisco Pizarro
as per his exploration incentive
simply quote "springs a trap"
for the Emperor of the Incas
Atahualpa –
under the aegis of Charles the Fifth of Spain
Holy Roman Emperor
Pizarro quote "springs a trap on the
Incan Emperor, Atahualpa"
quote from History dot com:

>"With fewer than 200 men against
>several thousand"
>Pizarro. the Catholic Explorer,
>lures the Incan Emperor Atahualpa
>quote "to a feast in the Emperor's honor
>and then opens fire on unarmed Incans."

Our Spanish Conquistador, under the aegis
of Charles the Fifth, Emperor of the Holy Roman
Empire and King of Spain quote
"opens fire on unarmed Incans"
and then his men quote "massacre
the Incans and capture Atahualpa
forcing him to convert to Christianity"
quote "before eventually killing him."

Quoting myself "as I am now
benefactor of quiet and a pen and notebook"
blessed beyond reason on this day just
before its dawn when this human species
centuries ago, as now
guided by an authoritarian
would and can slaughter those who
don't believe as they, the know-it-alls, believe.

    Mother of my night, what reflections
    in peaceful mind produce
    with the aid of facts
    never to be ignored or forgiven
    or forgotten – planet energies
    of peace and struggle provide
    only with respectful humility.
    Some care to care as the night provides.

SPIRIT LOSS

Spirit flows into the concrete night
into the plastic formations that cough up themselves
    into smaller irritants.
All the ugly chemical compositions that refuse to relate –
polystyrene foam, polyethylene, listen heartily,
glass can be reused but lectures seem to do no good.
The only safe good is avoidance, as I almost cut myself
scissoring and trying to pull the intense plastic off
    the batteries I just bought – *if Spirit enters such*
        obnoxious objects it has nowhere to go.
Why list the billions trillions of man-perfected objects
that resist and refuse the pathways of the Earth as if
they are to make their own self-inherited world
in an immense glob of death, a Borg glut? The forever
expanding useless hindrance, the fatal collection
    of everything gone wrong.

BRAIN WEATHER

Rained on by my thoughts
the turmoil from the cavern of my skull –
who deposits all of you there
    me, everything, a few taps from beyond?
The gush of gone things people landscape
close inspections, storm after storm of
    days and dreams
mists of remembered and forgot
clouds of known, cloud bursts and
    peaceful skies
frightful storms of the hateful but also
fair weather friends continuing alive –
in a glorious nurturing as if I'm just the earth
    needing you.

NO ROPES ATTACHED

Love supposes no ropes attached
no lariat surprise out of the night
no hug me and leave me but hug me and stay.
Let's work it out day by day.

    Love supposes the roses will come back
        after the winter
    and bloom when they bloom
        and dust when they dust.

Love is the most you can count on
    when there's the least to say,
the bond that returns when
    you thought it was frayed –
that is when it was built
    in more than a day.

    Love is the giving when needed the most
        over time
    fills the way to a better past,
    a partnership that refuses to bust
    or won't when given some trust.

Love is the practical heart to heart
buddy to buddy, art to art,
ear to voice and mind to mind.

    Love is body caring the most
        when weak and pale
    and holding up no room to fail.

Love supposes it arose
to be what you make it
to let it be free
and not mistake it.

THE ELEMENTS OF LOVE

The fires that leap love
the water that evaporates into it
the ground that is the ground for it
the air that forms the words for it
the circle that is its binding
the old stories that give it substance
the lips that form its magic heart
the eyes that see through it to its expanding core
the ears that hear songs it continually creates
the hormones it dictates to and then grows through
the lingering message it leaves in the mind from
   loves past gone
the form it takes to be a force
the space it lives in
the spirit of its sound of voice
the silence it comes out of and enters
   as it comes out now in a heart to heart talk
the hands held before and behind touching
   and remembered
the weight of its weightlessness
 the solidity of its force
  the attractiveness of its stories that become
     real life over time sooner or later,
        hopefully sooner
  the time that is now in all its forms.

TIMETABLE

"Out of the new comes the beginning of the old
as a beginning is constant so is the ending
as all the business of now going on seems
   wide and tall and huge and overpowering.
It isn't but an instant less than an instant in the overall
   the unseeable beginnings and possible endings
      of everything in and of *itself*."
         (Sayeth the Wormy Philosopher)

BEAUTIFUL NATURE

What is prominent
in the annoyed aftermath
of the future?
Well, gullible whales thinking plastics are
krill.
Bees adjusting to pesticide-ridden flowers
and dying of, *as we know.*
Humans, all except the rich,
turning into migrants.
Polar bears too warm to live calling out
to the past
layer on layer of life forms succumbing
to the results of human greed
and lack of action.
Mother Earth forced to act up to evacuate the culprit,
sending disease and drought out
to the self-righteous self serving
resource-destroying baby worshiping
self-preening homo sapiens –
their post future in Nature, *dominant* Nature
in the new healing era of Beautiful Earth.

EMPTY FOR YOU

Love admits its capacity to fill and fill and fill
as long as it's not crowded out by noise, garbage, and baloney.
As long as it's not strong-armed out by steel testosterone.
As long as there's room for it to bloom
an emptied out open mindedness,
an honest willingness to receive.

FOOL

It must be time as time again times us –
thrilling gesture of the Fool who
abandons the King to live out a hermit's life,
there where time doesn't matter,
there among all the fighting infants.
"They'll never grow up,," the Fool says as he
kicks them out the door, all of them armored up
    and carrying guns.
"I like to be alone," he says, "to watch the sunset,
to be alive and breathe when the Sun comes up –
the only ruling master of the unruly Earth babies
    the de-evolved, the little rugrats of human beings.
But little do they care about anything but their toys."
The Fool could be the last adult on Earth
in my picture of animal and plant hopelessness.
Admired in his house, just trying to be alone
    with his candle.

S acred
O pen
B eautiful
R eal
I maginative
E nlightening
T hankful
Y es
    - anonymous

TEACHERS

Mother of Right-Wrong, the ankles and wrists of know-how
the speed reading of inspiration, the voice of follow along,
    of saying and believing
the caricature of heart and then the real heart –
you reflect the gift given whether good or bad
but then in intellect and dividing direction, you correct
    what can be corrected.
Slow learning you can speed as everything goes out of control
    in your control.
Mother of the Good-Bad, the good gods gone bad,
retrieve, ease, restore, filling the cups with recuperation
ancient turning of cool-down restored, a possibility
in your non-body hands, in your dreaming energies
    slow to be formed, unformed, as cycles cycle out
and the healing hospital bed turns into a view of the sunset
with dawn on the other side of you coming around
rising out of nowhere the energy of youth turned into
    caretakers, sparking awe and service
to the Mother of restorative wisdom, singing voice of
    education,
where the teachers are plants and animals, all the nonhuman
    wisdom wrapped into one.
Mother of holding-breath-together whispers voices song –
Know-how of Earth Spirits, your children all in choruses,
    teaching the humans.

MOUSETRAP - A POEM FOR LEVI ROMERO
(It comes from the flesh and the bones, the blood and the soul.)

The entire history of the Arts is at stake.
All the musicians who've played for kings and even tyrants
while often cutting them down to size,
their voices of Peace, raptures of Love, stories of the Oldest
    Songs on Earth they sacrificially keep alive
        all those strains of beauty,
    are on the verge of destruction.
And the arts, even cave arts, return to total
    uninterrupted darkness.

That is in the despotic nightmare already here,
    with martial songs of praise ,
    large smiling billboards of the Leader,
the loud lying Leader who is "Presidente de las Artes."

The avant garde is dead as it was but now *must* be –
    freedom impossible but for
voices of acceptance of repression.
The dour, the dismal, and the dead live –
freedom to *lie* in unamused acceptance,
the hand of painters in grip of the controller –
free speech is the speech of the dead, the vision
from the brush and hand of the artist
    in chains of revisionism
spouting messages of the mighty oligarchs,
    the *wealthy* beyond
imagination of anyone ordinary,
as women are pushed back in the kitchens of the dull
    and controlled by numbed men.

Art is drained from imagination
    theater of commercials the only drama –
actors, robots of the wealthy, dancers imitating
    movements of mindless minds propagating "happiness"
the sense of art and freedom and creative discourse.

    Humane humanity
is crushed by greed and coercion
    the muscular force of dominance –
    ritualized repetitive behavior with loud bands
and marching clones.

"Creativity is destruction" - " lies are the mind's eye"
conforming gestapo moving you to death's door
authoritarian boot crushing art *out*,
    and that goes with history, no history
        but the story of a canned Hell
which is what is here, what is coming when speech
    and song and display are denied freedom.
And women, all colors of the human species
    all sexual love and yearnings are warped
        and molded to the exact cadence of
feudal subjugation from the rich and powerful: SO
this you *must* say: "One and only one, I love you,
you are my source of everything I follow –
    my mind after yours. You have everything!
        I have nothing except from your bountiful grace
            that allows me to grovel before you
                quiet
                    as a mouse."

I DON'T LIKE YOU

The head of my heart burst
since you trampled my era.
My rose developed a fistula
and my ducks squawk.
Everything turned upside down
and developed a stench.

"POOTIN"

a poophead   a putrid
a pill-head   plop
a pimp   a pack
a prick   of puke
                    a pate
a pin-head   of hate
a pip   a Nazi
a pap   of nuts
a pandemic   a criminal
                    muss
a pomp   a ghastly
a piss   result
a pea-brain   of the Devil's
a puss   pus.

GUNS GALORE

"Too many guns, too many guns
all the US has too many guns -
guns in the belfry, guns in the bath
guns in the bedroom to kick your ass.

     Guns in your vest, guns in your boots
     guns in your pocket so you have to shoot.
     Need more guns? 3D-printer-at home
     print out a ghost gun source unknown.

Too many guns, too many guns
all the US has too many guns -
guns in the living room, guns in the car
guns on the brain wherever you are."
                         /Easter Morning

CARRIER

Though I walk through the shadow of the value of stealth
I will find no answer till the blind speak through cemented mouths
    and the furniture of vacant houses returns
to keep me company in this deaf paradise.
Knees won't bend to pray if you can't get up.
The human kiss has become a puncture
    and the eyes gouge you out.
Lead me from the coercion of any church
and back to bringing some water to the scorched earth.

HEART TO HEART

    "Have heart to heart talk with yourself.
    Yes your true self has a heart too.
     Are you in alignment
      at least enough to see eye to eye
       beat to beat in an embrace
        or are you at a distance
         stubbornly apart?

      "Your true self is aware of the misery
       the suffering, the unconditional unnecessary pain
      but also the valor, the courage,
     the will to live a good life on a planet already
    harmed by lack of respect and love for its bounty
and its creative diversity that needs its own space.

"The heart of the planet is still beating.
  Are you still in alignment with it
   your true self and yourself?
    Or are you all three so dispersed
     you're falling apart?
    It is possible to have a heart to heart talk
   with yourself and the planet which is
  the source of all truth. Here."

AND THEN THERE'S PUTIN

                                (BOOM)   *(deep drum)*
Bashar al-Assad, all lying aside
awaiting war crime accountability
delayed by vetoes Russia and China
    in sympathy with,
Assad and his criminal chemical agents
deadly sarin and chlorine *barrel bombs*   *(sar-in)*
turning innocent civilians into gasping
    flat laid out dead women
        men children.
Assad killed thousands also, also in
    mass hangings!
ANY opposing him or *suspected of protest*
handcuffed, tortured, how about boiling water
    poured on you repeatedly?
Among a thousand other atrocities
bearing the Badge of Impunity –
Assad's administered deaths in Syria 600,000
though the *children* only 25,000 – Impunity Reigns
in the Dictatorial Sport.
And then there's Putin.   *(BOOM)*

Omar al-Bashir, during 30 year dictatorSHIT   *(al-ba*shee*r)*
led a war in Darfur region with only hundreds
    of thousands smashed dead, millions
        displaced away –
welcomed in his friend Osama bin Laden
sent thousands including child soldiers
    to fight in Saudi Arabia's Yemen War.
In Darfur of Sudan he displaced innocents *by force*
using rape as weapon of war,
    aerial bombing campaigns - sound familiar?
        His metier
genocide. Bashir living in contempt
    of the International Criminal Court,
        a stunning victory for Impunity –
the Devastator of Sudan
    and de-stabilizer of countries surrounding –
        just
    crimes against *humanity.*

And then there's Putin.   *(BOOM)*

Stalin, Mao Zedong, Batista, Saddam Hussein,
    Mobutu Sese Siko, Haji Muhammad Suharto
and then there's Putin.   *(BOOM)*

Pol Pot
forced Cambodia into agrarian socialist
    society – it only took up to two million
deaths – only a quarter of the population
    to wipe out *opposition*.
Backed by his buddy Mao Zedong and the Chinese   (Tse*Tong*)
    Communist Party
to the tune of a billion dollars' worth of aid
his Khmer Rouge emptied cities and forced ALL
to country labor camps – just took
    mass executions, forced labor, abuse abuse
        every kind of abuse
and disease to get the people to comply – plus
    196 prisons.
Hardly any survivors, the Killing Fields
    over 200,000 dead, skulls and bones.
 Pol Pot, at least *he* was convicted of treason
    by his own colleagues and died.
Then there is Putin.   *(BOOM)*

Pervez Musharrof, Muammar Gaddafi,   (Pervaze Mu*har*rof)
Mengistu Haile Mariam, Idi Amin.   (men*gis*-too holly mahr-ee-um)
                                      (eedee ameen)
Lon Nol, Robert Mugabe, Kim Jong-un   (mu-gob-ay)
and then there's Putin.   *(BOOM)*

Impunity reigns in the Dictatorial Sport,
a game to the sick egotistical martial mind
the steel claw for power and fame
but to everyone else and the bombarded planet
ongoing pain.

And then there's Putin.   *(BOOM)*

PORTRAIT OF THE MIRROR
(As an agent of the FBI)

"I see you but you may not see me until the
 prongs of the Great Fork are visible and that
  can't be possible because God is a sissy
 and doesn't like to play with forks.
He's definitely a spoon man.
So I can observe at my pleasure or my disgust
all your petty goings on and your secret encounters
 with the devil in your pitiful spirit, those few of you
  who conspire with your sick selves to take
   over the world. No dog has nine lives and you,
    you dog, are dead. I have secret weapons at
     my disposal and secret loves if you kiss
      the mirror, right, right there."

DARK OPERA

The fractured element of debacle
    stares us in the face
as Wagner plays on with his harps and horns
    an ending of his massive
propaganda mythology
    the spewing of ego wastes
nationalist pigheadedness
    in the rising volumes of the dark opera –
is this bliss to kiss ourselves
    if we are the right race
let everybody produce babies
    and burn up the trees
which are the last cooperative minds alive
as we mono-materialists, oil crazed and unhappy,
give up our human rights to the insects.

"This is Placiditas?"

TRUST SONG

"I offer my heart to sing with –
a duo would be nice don't you think?
Maybe a trio if there's someone you trust.
Isn't trust the secret of the song in heart?
Who are we anyway if not a chorus?
You and me, someone to trust within
and without?
More and more people depopulate the human spirit
but we trust together and sing accordingly
a chord of three maybe four notes I can't help it
I'm at the piano again, are you listening?
Oh, you're singing now and I'm playing!"

RAIN RUN RAW WATER

Rain run raw water
the Tingling Gods are pleased –
Old Wind Woman of the Mountain
blowing clouds wet dispersed
blunder bumping booming overhead
the Howling Twins
as the vertical army of drops
take peaceful conquest –
suffering plants bathed like no other
accurate smell floats up from the
parched utterly baked too long standing Earth
Rain Gods blown up from Aztec ruins
attending Spider Woman here
in the cottonwood root in the Altar in the study –
unstudies to *release* all concentration
Clay Bowl four-cornered, wet
corresponding above in the wet wind
in the slow almost all night thunderless
Blessing . . . *rain run raw water* . . . .

MOTHER OF GOD

What happened to your Son?
Haven't heard much lately –
just a bunch of questionable disguises
popping up and assuming power to control,
nothing but coercive pop ups
clinging to more and more masculine
and not so beneficial control.
　　What is *your* stance, Mother of God
now Mother of a bunch of spinoffs
from the Real Thing, a bunch of *pre*tends
with hateful power and ugly presence –
　　what went wrong and poisoned character?
This offshoot from Mother Earth
that gave rise to such privileged hope?

SUPREME COURT PROHIBITS SPERM FREEDOM

"Supreme Court overturns freedom of ejaculation before marriage for men. Men can not now ejaculate till marriage and then only within a woman for (sacred) procreation. The States must set up sperm banks in every city to contain accidentally or illegally ejaculated sperm. The individual fine and imprisonment for men who break the law by ejaculating sperm before legal marriage will be determined by each state. Male sperm is the issue of God and since it is half the life of a baby it is sacred life and the property of the government until the holy gates of marriage are opened. It is sacred as is the female egg and must not be killed but given continued life. Sperm Police will work with State Police to arrest non-married ejaculators and gather their sperm for the banks.

Signed: Justice Kneel Gore-Suck, Justice Brat Cave-a-Naught, Justice Amy Conehead, Justice Samuel In-Darko and Justice Pubic Hair Thompson."
　　　　Reporter: Lorenzo Garbanzo, Placiditas, New Mexico

"HAVE MERCY ON MY SOUL"

"It's a paltry thing. You can see it there kind of ragged
    just hovering there somewhere below
or you can see it up there
    like a tattered kite barely holding together
        as if it's ready to slowly fall apart
            pieces scattered in this wind
and/or it lands on the table, fragmented
    as if it's asking for something, water?
No, that would drown it, substance? food?
        tending of some sort? but I don't know how to
            tend to it –
    beef it up, give it vitamins, pray to it?
I need a soul doctor. Maybe he'll just
let it be and see where it shows up next
    if it show up at all."

DRY APHRODITE

"I don't remember anything about
                the press of fire against my chest
the whirling down of water from Zeus
            but now relaxed, repaired
I've swelled into the beauty I always was
                and here to serve that young man over there
as a guide of *ferocious* beauty demanding
           unending tenderness."

MIND ROT

Be the glacier dissolving in my blood
the Polar Bear pacing in my brain looking
    for snow and ice,
the fish and birds gagging in my veins on
    infinite particles of plastic debris
the storm's heat waves rising, seas warming
invading my mind filling it with regrets (too late)
the flooding mold impact disease and drowning
as I try to cough it out, stuck in my gut glutting
    my throat hacking hacking no avail
I bend over exhausted suffering heatstroke
feeling the burning pain on verge of heart attack
chemical hazards unknown seep through dirt
as mosquitoes swarm and I'm trying to
    brush off ticks.
The people around me moving in, raiding
    what I have left, the yard swelling
with invasive plants, lionfish and cockleburs
    the water left I try to drink acidic
the dead coral scraping my flesh as I
    lie down, trying to eat the dead spoiled fish.

CONTENT

Life brings light into the writing
    through the sound and movement of
        the pen on the paper, the energy of
            the hand and mind together, pushing
        and releasing, hearing coming through –
    the words connecting, the revealed content.

MORE THAN ONCE THE STARS

More than once the stars threatened to poke me
and the trippy tune on the radio was like darts of laughter.
"The joke's on you," said the retarded pig
    supposedly penned up in the living room
so I went outside to stare at the goons
        hanging out there
but nobody there but the cool air of late summer
and Jupiter bright in the sky staring me down
    asking
"And what have *you* contributed to
    mytholo*geee*?"

NEW MEXICO SONG

Correct me if I'm wrong
    elevate my song
        to a pattern of joy
      like a landscape of interbeings
    interspersed cooperative
  in working peace
that rests into itself, as itself
where joy is simply the juice of energy
  slow breathing ignites
    the power factory of the universe
      at peace at peace at peace
      at peace in the landscape
        where everybody includes plants
      everybody is plants, and the River
        the center of the State we evolve from
    if our peaceful surprise is up to it
our peaceful surprise.

WHAT HAPPENED TO THE SONNET

What happened to the sonnet, someone said
writing one anyway – nothing gets exhausted
since it's cyclical – what comes around numbs around
if you know what I mean, so saying it again
is how you say it, not what dish is left unwashed.
Oh I see, nostalgia will keep bringing something up
just so you can have the same worn-out experience again
so you might as well write a limerick if you
know how to rhyme and tell dirty jokes
or why not a sonnet with new rules of course –
the same ones you used before when you wrote
two years of them, that is, anything with 14 lines
   some of them skinny, some of them run-on fat
   and guess what before you know it that's where you're at.

FIRST STEP

      What happened to the joy, the glee
     the jumping up and down with delight oh!
    The legs hurt too much, the progress is too slow
   just getting up from a chair, the impetus to do
is a little weak, is almost not there, sitting
staring into space, what an occupation! But
the undone things piled up, turn to fantasies you
can stare at, baffled, where the inertia?
There must be movement first, movement first,
 strain and pull up not necessarily at 'em
 but the precious activity of going through those
 family high school histories letters photos where
to put them? Give them to someone *else* not as connected
to dispose of, hurrah! I've done one thing – they're
   off the shelf.

FIRE FLOOD – DEATH OF THE OLIGARCHS

The flood fueled the fire which knocked out
the transmission lines and the torrential undergrowth
devastated the top of the hurricane and dislodged
the underpinning of the Earth as drought upended
the avalanche forming uninhabitable patches larger
than the Pacific – meanwhile the earthquakes
joined forces and divided the North from the South
the East from the West as pestilence set in and
viruses escaped from the infected humans to
all the animals of the Earth causing a rare pause
to the invasion of the Nato states from the Russian Oligarch
Goon Squad as the last hospital was submerged in
the upperclass filth from yacht fever and mansion poison
devastating fire flaming forth sparking the last ember
    skyward.

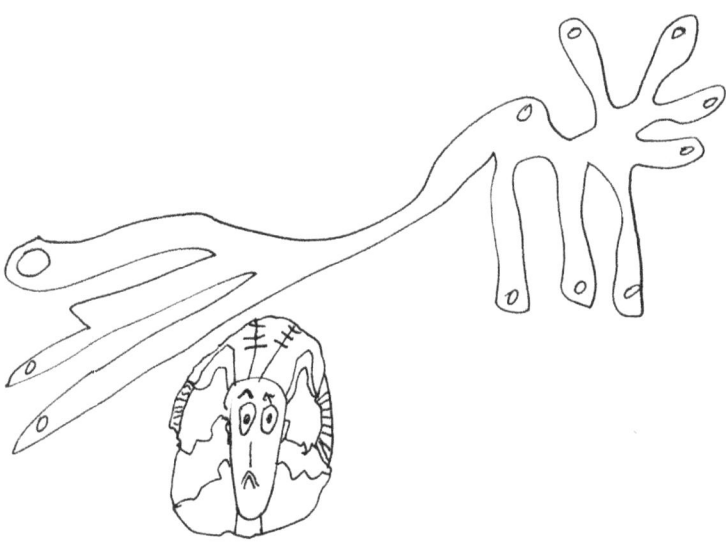

THE SYRINGE WARTS HAVE COME TO TOWN

Everybody knows what they are – oh there's one! Just step over it.
The last time I saw one was in April or was it in November when
I threw my old dictionary away.

THE TRUMPETA LINE!

"Nothing does it like *Trumpeta* –
for the ultimate turn off at your next
    post-punk party!
Buy *Trumpeta*.
Trumpeta comes in 3 exotica colors
    chunky or smooth.
It's flexible and adheres to anything.
It disgusts the toughest type
    and jars the rigidly jaded.
Trumpeta Plus, our Fancy Gold line,
comes with a full array of textural effects
    and is instantly expandable
to fit *any* post-punk occasion.
Disgust the sox off your friends
    and be the Puke-King of the Party!
Buy *Trumpeta* or *Trumpeta Plus*
    with living multiple accessories."

HIGH MEADOW

The light fine dusting of the soul
brings memory back, lost treasures of reading
    far into the exploring night –
each page a cure all to the need to know
    what soothes afflictions,
    what brings water to the soul,
    dryness to the lips to want more.
The words ignite imagination, satisfaction
and that sickness now is repaired, a new door opened
    on peace, every peaceful field imaginable – wild
geraniums, morning glories, asters, emerging cosmos
yarrow abrupt, verbena tall species, milkweed startling
    red orange, hooker's primrose and wall flower
reaching up as the old books and newer brought me to
this healing place, this mixture transporting through to
    something new.

SEVENTIES BROTHER

At the high foothills of North Sandia Mountain,
Holy Man who with your jay tail-feathered staff
    glides out (walks through) . . .
    Today I have become trustful of,
    Today I look to you for help.

But there's only your Staff and Digging Sticks
in the abandoned garden.

OFFHAND HEALING

      What can bring your hurt out and away?
   The body seems not to compromise with pain,
the doctors, rare to see, reaching the blockage
    they don't seem to know,
the powerful images on their screens tell them one thing,
    your body tells you another.
                  What is to say, what is to do?
The hands of healing, where are they, the ancient connections
    the lifting of touch into a sky of reprieve,
        a stability of peace, a reflection of creative energy,
           a restoration and beyond, a balanced clearer
        way of life. Oh release, oh relief, oh mystery light
           into daily alertness, fresh movement of limbs
    and ease of following through purpose,
        sound living free of striking pain, the gift
           that should be life's
    working through the demands of work, pleasurably.

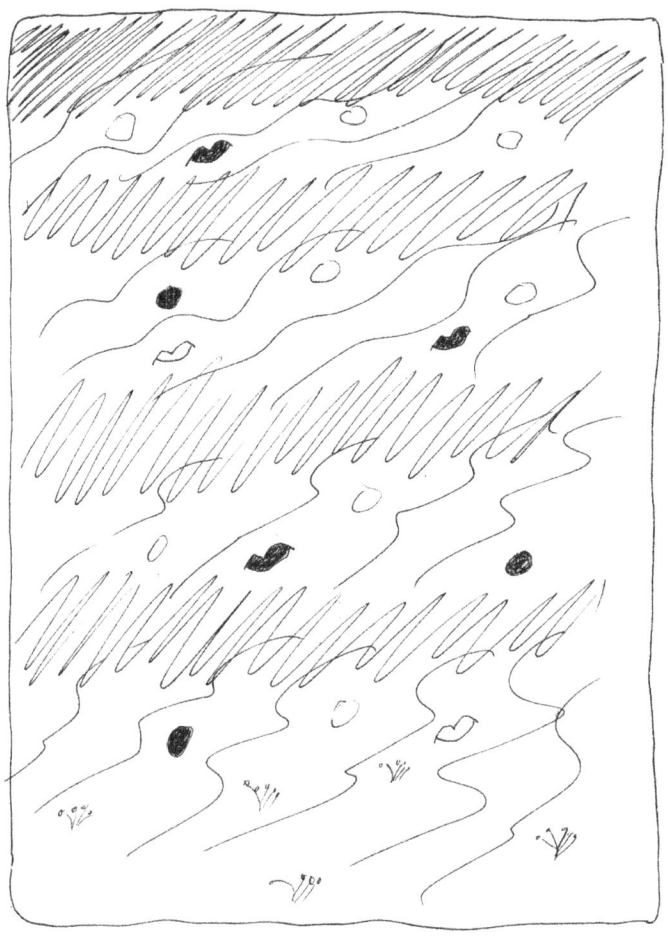

85+

    Time has ripped fabric
from my mind
that held together
my connection to the stars.

    Now the connection
comes infrequently
as if through a lens
dimly.

CARE

As the time gets dark and chaos whips up energy
foul forked-tongued treachery shreds at Democracy.
The basest ego surrounds itself with ass-kissers
and powerful providers tilting everything toward
    strong-arm control
and the flatterers, lily-livered, sitting on their posh toilets,
command the treason dance, the tearing down of diversity,
the religious frenzy of control and kill to be alike.

I'm not like any of you as the Earth commands in my veins,
my heart containing all energy of its past
the soft sensitive love of amazing renewing,
the mind of compassion and soul of equal opportunity
leading the body to *cooperative* community,
    the *commons* of love and work, voice of the creative,
honor of respect for multiplicity, love and care
where the Mountains, Rivers, Fields, all Creatures of Nature
    hold sway in diversity everywhere.

RELATIONS

Don't you believe it? It is so true. You *can* get through.
There's a giving up in the release, the release, the release
as if falling without going any place, the kiss from an Aunt
who always seemed starchy, now recuperating and sweet
as she always was, had you seen. To see through your own
clawing demands. All this accumulated stuff to be done
like weights, all around holding you down – the Uncle
you *could* have known better, the one with opposing politics –
he was smart and a source of family history, all these
enriching souls you do know, do know of, your tired energy
doesn't let you reach out, reconnect, take advantage of the given!
A family of possibilities you let go by, which, just reaching out,
you could get through anything and, not too late, build health
and relate, *relate*.

T-I-T-U-S

> "Nothing surprises any more.
> It's the same old culture of guns –
> Pow! you're dead, and I didn't do it.
> I'll gladly go without food for kids
> so I can buy expensive bullets.
> What? over 2 bucks each and I need a lot
> for target practice.
> I like to go out and scare those people with
> their cameras looking for flowering plants.
> RAT-A-TAT TAT in big letters.
> Titus for Trump. Trump taught us
> Titus Andronicus – T-I-T-U-S
> *Trump Insurgency in The United States,*
> Tight with Titus the Be All and End All.
> I like to pepper Nancy Pelosi targets with fancy bullets.
> I'm tight with Trump's Insurgency In The United States.
> TITUS for all, Titus Andronicus."
>
> /thanks to Malcolm Nance for "T I T U S"

"In Titus Andronicus, Shakespeare's bloody revenge tragedy, they're burned alive, arms chopped off, son stabbed by father, the murdered thrown into a pit, the woman raped hands cut off tongue cut out, two men decapitated, nurse and midwife stabbed, a clown executed for no reason, two killed and cooked in a pie and fed to the mother, Titus then kills two woman, is killed and the killer killed, a man is buried up to his neck and left to starve and a woman thrown out to the wild beasts."

INEVITABILITY?

Can a real insurgency happen without
    severed heads and arms
        and tongues cut out,
women raped and men full of nothing but revenge?
Yes, by vote.

AIR

What lifts the most enlightened turning point,
even *that* up?
Sky descends, Earth rises, a "now" in a breath
somewhere between good and bad, sad and rad.
What element of art or living
lifts up that heaviness of body, tiredness,
inertia standstill?
The birds of early morning not yet to sing.
What is *that?* The neighbor's rooster
and bird songs from the classical station
to announce a new unsponsored morning
this August 16th when you know what happened 1896?
Gold discovered in the Klondike. Oh that rush that
subsequent rush. Thich Nhat Hahn not yet to say
"breathe in, breathe out," and, I say,
think what you're breathing, *air* –
you're just part of earth.

RETRIBUTION FROM FIRE

Echo tostada. Fires in the fire.
The fire I started as a kid
in back of the Philips 66 gas station
on Main Street in Roswell.
The oil pit went up in smoke.
Things get pretty hot
when you get spanked.

USELESSNESS

I keep praying to an afterthought that used to be
    a forethought and before that was
the only thought
    and now all I have are the arrears
of regrets that all those thoughts had no ears.

DIAGNOSIS

"My feet are unstuck marbles and my toenails are lust.
My kidneys are bipolar, my heart has the touch.
The flower garden in my brain cells lifts in latitude.
My arrangement for scheduling a doctor's appointment
    is well in hand as the palms create thrust.
The stars of my peppered clouds produce a broken rainbow.
Driving back from the hallucination of bolts
    my hardware store collapsed into a sea of mud
    where the seeds of hundred year old native plants sprouted.
As my time turned to injury my doctor turned into space.
Thrust and gravity combined in a pitched economy.
Ouch said the classical radio as my pants went north.
Be where you are, my mother said to my entire lack of direction –
    pray and you won't get more rouge in your cheeks.
My knees are a whirling dervish of paralyzed enlightenment."

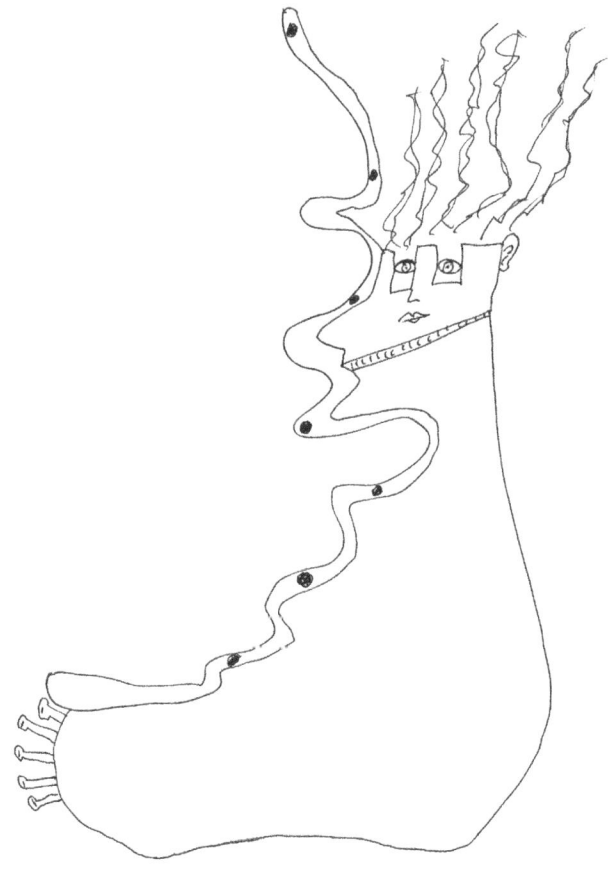

FLYSWATTER

Do you time your light by fires of the Right
    plunged into the calculation of destruction
        ending the face of history with a puke and a hanging?
So the only noise you make is firecrackers and cherry bombs
    and to hell with the Fountain of Venus?
Has your masculine stance stuck rods in your pants
    and armor imbedded in your tattooed skin
        your antiquated so-called religion a rape
    of a Middle East prophet
to your ends of guns, weapons, to quote "protect"
    your core of feverish fear, in fact
        a whole arsenal of fear your protective gear –
proud gang members of the idiotic fringe now
    parading in public hate-flags and insignia
from the worst poison of rotten bollocks history.

May the feminine hand of reduction come down
    like a flyswatter on your 6-legged
        hatred of democracy as
you wriggle back to some normalcy of love and cooperative
    Spirit!

Don't worry.
The night will be
all light in the morning.

RAD WAY

I don't want to dwell on the bad,
I want the good to be rad.

SONG OF DIVERSITY

   The song song songs of *many* spirits
 the freshness of difference, the startling feast
  you encounter just around the corner
you never knew existed, with its carnival of music –
music be the soul of every life alive in new
   and renewing musicians, the song that sings
    and plays in many souls.
Creativity the air that breathes, the colors of skin
   that sing, the many many differences –
       culture cultures,
    food foods,
   story stories all risen
from foundations of Planet Earth, Earth Earths –
the evolution of tree spirits, foundation roots,
   sea and air into life, life lives lives in
creative mystery of the song story dance
    within the holding of Earth measure.
Music and musicians the magical peaceful language
  of diversity and diversities.

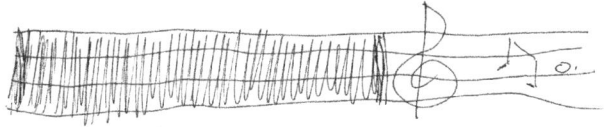

GENERATIONS

The generations of hands in one hand.
With your generations of feet have walked here.
With your generations of minds have thought
 your way here.
With your generations of hearts have worked and
 felt your way here.

THE OBVIOUS

We're all going up in a puff of Oil
with Tyrants trying to take over every patch of freedom
but at the same time we can meet it with compassion
and the love that keeps each of us doing the right thing.
There is the Earth renewing renewing renewing
    in spite of the extremes we force it into.
There's the cosmos, geraniums, yarrow, buckwheat,
    mint and more – cosmos, cosmos
        by the diminishing stream
right here in Las Huertas Canyon – the willow
hawthorn aspen and the suffering pines
but the Earth of it all will continue in spite of
the fetus-worshipers of our Species that's multiplied
    4 *times* since my birth in 1935.
Religions that worship the human body as God
and the billion billionaires hoarding their secrets
    in their rapacious mansions –
but we can take a deep breath and celebrate
    all the good we can do, the Music, and the Art
        and Love for each other.

!

EVIL

    Evil is more difficult to deal with
        than good to be.
    Evil is interior and expresses itself
        outward as the good to be
    which expresses itself downward
    and holds in power the evil degree.

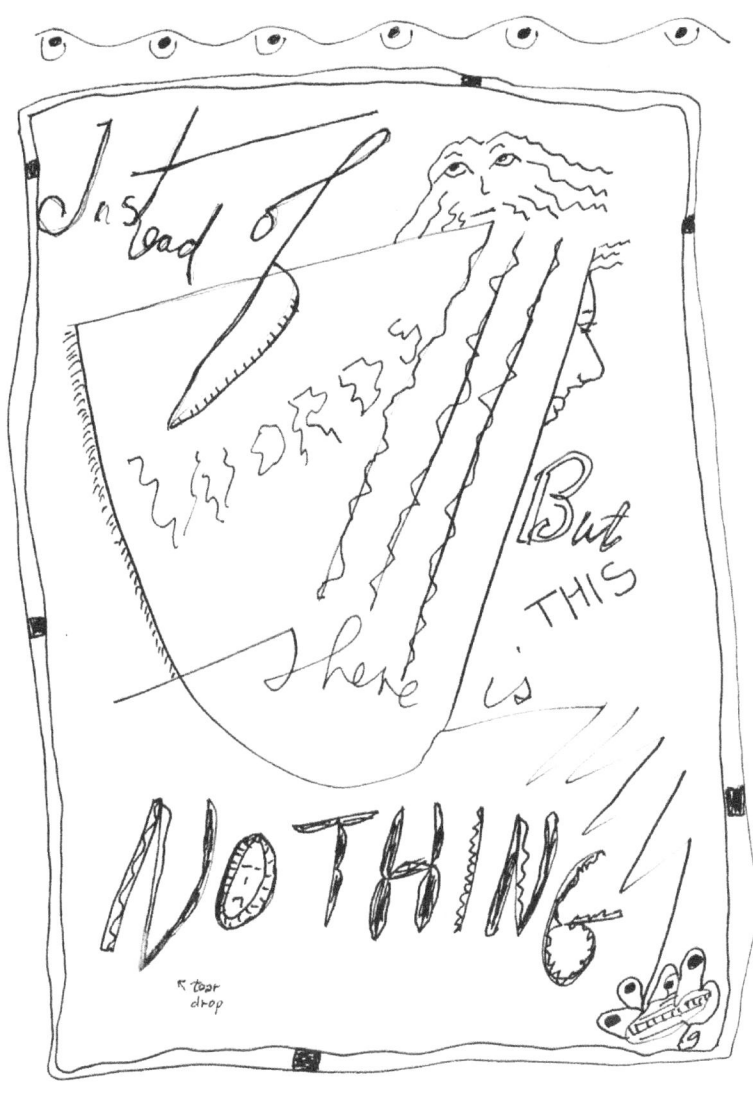

IMPOSSIBILITY OF ESCAPE

> Stars are after me
> Heavens join the chase
> I run like a dog but
> the Cosmos devours me.

"EVEN THE DOGS"

There are too many people in the world
and humans are manipulators
trying to manipulate the Earth
and the Earth burns back.

There's no such thing as nationalism
only Earthism
but human groups are too greedy
to realize the truth.

Manipulation to get more
as trillionaires manipulate the billionaires
who manipulate, that is,
MAN-ipulate the millionaires
and all MAN-ipulate
those below
on down to the guy
who can't afford
their inflated prices
and has to work all day
and sleep on the streets at night
    where, as he says,
"Even the dogs wee wee on me."

MOMENTARY RELEASE INTO NOW

Arising from the pain into the light of love
the laugh in free heart, the careful ease
of smooth working joints and reliable body.
Sensuous pleasure of just being.

SERPENT MEDITATION

I entered the Mosque of my mind
 the Cavern of Solitude
  the rare fission of energy
  relaxed
   slow
       movement to be still
        I *retreated* –
          there was that small empty church
          there was the chambers of the monastery
          the garden with artificial ferns
          the pool run by a small quiet motor
          with goldfish and minnows
         and then the thought of a cathedral come to me
         and I entered it –
    no one was there, nor was I.
  I entered *wishful* thinking
 but the wish dropped away
and the classical waltz came from
the radio, on low –

as I entered the cleavage of my bed
 and picked up the fishing pole someone
   had left right by the Jemez River
      and noticed there was no hook
  no bobbin at the end of the line.

   That's when I returned to my true home
     pre-dawn, light out
      in bed.
       The waltz was the waltz from "Der Rosenkavalier"
         written by *Ri*kard Strauss
          who said, after he shook Hitler's hand,
           "That was the happiest day of my life."
         A wonderful old Viennese woman
           on the second floor of Doheny Library
         at University of Southern California
         told this to me, and ever since . . .
       no *Ri*kard for me.

WINTER SOLSTICE – PLACITAS

    Dim dark out there, already well past 6
    and I got to bed so early just to get warm –
    turning off the carols from the classical station –
    don't need sappy birth music,
        for when was Jesus born   anyway?
      And thinking him or any human as god absurd to me,
        and insult to the wonderful animals/creatures
          who are our neighbors on Earth, their spirits, too.

  And ALL this stuff, the entire trappings is basically
  a terrifying journey of loss of light, darkest day today,
  with the only hope the turning around the sun to appear, more
  and more each day, the celebration of so-called Christians.
  I have no connection with Middle Eastern shenanigans, if
  I have any respect and empathy it's for the nearby growth up
     from our American Earth here – place determines spirituality
        and even religion and not the reverse – to me.

Native American Hopi Pueblo Navajo respect and working with
     Mother Earth and Father Sun – that makes close sense.
Buddha can transcend boundaries since he never claimed god level.
The ancient Hanukkah lights transcend, blessing light as a miracle
     even Einstein professed the wonder of.
  May it prosper the Sun and our cockeyed Earth in meaningful
       juxtaposition/partnership.
   As the dance between light and water leads us to Spring.
     Welcome brightening day and health to our deep need,
       well health.

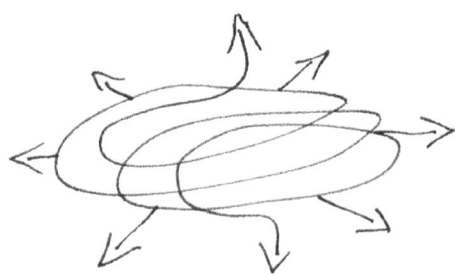

ZELENSKYY AND COMPATRIOTS

Zelenskyy and compatriots and (most) Americans
    for freedom of speech
    separation of church and state
    freedom of choice
Zelenskyy and compatriots and (most) Americans
    for Democracy
    the Constitution
    all people created Equal
    standing up for Individuality and
    the Common Good
    and not caving to any
        tyrant.
Zelenskyy and compatriots and (most) Americans
    for creativity, new ideas, science
        compassion, music above all
            and the arts
in interchange of problem-solving
    and work and trade
and freedom of spirit of mind and history.

SOURCE

    On higher power
        on higher empathy
       the valleys of Nepal
      echoing deep throated
      control relaxed in the transported
      sound
       that carries carries
     worldwide to here and back in
    appreciation
    the healing sound you can hear even
   if you can hear nothing
   comes into the ears the ears of the mind
  the mind of open hearing
 when healing is hearing
the sound over the landscape
the landscape of sound
of the rolling hills the echoing valleys –

it must come from afar
from the deepest cosmos
the cosmos of earth
of sacred regions
the holiest ghost of healing
soul spirit in the voice
from Nepal from Mount Taylor
      (which is Turquoise)
from the flat out mountain
   and deep sea
the ocean's rolling sound
carries the breath of origin
from the sacred mountains
across and to here.

It is the breath of vibrant spirits
 the breath of beings of transport
  that bring the values of earth with them
   the breath of sound judgment, sound balance
    powers contained in simplicity
    the evolution and being of health

    from Capitan, from Sierra Blanca
   from the Sandias, from Taylor
     the Sangre de Cristo and Wheeler

      from the hills that lead into mountains
      the living springs, the breath of fresh air
     connected even afar as Nepal
    and hear it as all voices hear it –
   it is simply the coordination of the four points
   four spaces empty spaces being fulfilled,
  the powers of equal empathy
 filling what was empty with healing
as all is empty, to empty out to welcome
as all in every direction is simplified direction
to heal what is sick, relaxed in natural presence
when all is emptied out to allow
we allow, we welcome we welcome in from afar
all distance is new and the natural order speaks
hearing what it hears in the need for anewing
the power of balance and essence of nature
when not interfered but allowed in its power.
A higher empathy from the valleys and close hills.

We welcome in the Spirit of Knowing
 the breath behind each heart beat
  engaging us, we of the family of ourselves
   as part of the Earth as Earth is part of us
   sounding the sound of our hearing
    from every direction into one centered
     where there is no demand only acceptance,
      as this power flows in from afar and the nearest near
     bringing healing with it as in all of us –
    neighbors rocks mountains inhabitants
     the interconnected connected creatures loves
      friends family, the sickness being entered and released
     as release is relaxation and health, deep sounds
    that carry with it the baseline and foundation
        of the entered and explored directions –
   sunlight stars moon to quide by
  here on Earth in healthy satisfaction based on
 power that enters and succeeds, expressed by gratitude ➜

that is before that is through that is around and part
as part of is everything
going forward from the centering here
in thankful grace as it is freely given
and accepted
heard from all centers and hills and
places of valued source
having arrived here where those before us
can teach
and show us as our way reveals itself
before us around and in, in source
in health again.

FOR LENORE

When you are gone
long time seems longer.
How did we meet.
Artists.
We were not bankers
or we would never have met.
I thought your art was fantastic
groundbreaking
and you were intrigued by
my different approach
and more.
However and no matter what happened
we stayed together.
And here we are or would be
if you weren't out walking
and I worry
when I'm not with you.

Sky heart
envelope the playing part
that laugh that lifted
ever so short
saved the day
or at least the hour
between us.

I'M THE ME I WANT TO BE

Look it up Google the fool and write it down
just borrow and transcribe steal there's nothing
left of your brain but partridge no
    postage, rather porridge I mean mush.
    You've been staring at your selfie so long
    you don't know whether your legs are erased
or one is too long as you look up "legs"
and positions for being more attractive
gluing your false eyelashes on upside down
    as it doesn't matter since you can
    alter your selfie any way you want
    as your metal ears and nose clash
as you attempt to stare
through your black pancake make up
at the message you just got from
    the message you just sent Hello
    truly you, it's so cool to meet you again
    the nonstop nonthinking phone to myself
texting, you are so delicious having bought
52-50 perfume for the noisome crowd except
look up "crowd" what is that something to avoid
    keep it to your automatically appropriate
    self winning the lottery don't you wish
    the complete installation of a walk-in tub
for teenagers look it up stupid how old am I
I don't have to remember a thing
since I don't even know what organs
    are appropriate for me to look best the next time
    I ask myself or rather itself if I still
    have a body or did it fly to Mexico or did
that thing you saw on TV really exist I
just got half of my hair done lip red
and the other half clipped down to stubs of
    blue green there, my selfie mate just told me to
    cut the whole thing off but when I asked
    "what is life" in a loud voice that

got attention the thing crashed
and I couldn't face myself during the charge
which was only 5 minutes which was
    the worst experience of my life oh shit
    it's my birthday now what was I going
    to alter this time oh yeah that god thing
who the fuck is god and the pop ups
take over and there is no way out but
happy times and the showers of balloons
    that pop up in abundance every time I
    congratulate myself. There it goes
    again!

GLOOMY GLOOM

Gloomy gloom
looming
ballooning doom no room
    for festooning
    or trippy tuning
just a fuming
and the gloom.
    Oh doom –
    I beat your butt
with my broom.
    Get out of my
fine little room –
    no time to fume!
I'm quite content
without you.
    What good is a gloomy
goon?
    From what poisoned plot
have you been exhumed?

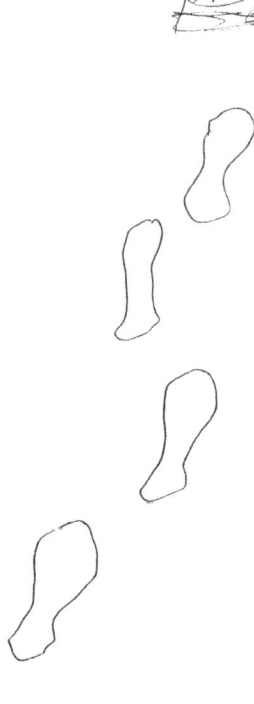

"MY RELIGION IS KINDNESS"
– Tenzin Gyatso, the 14th Dalai Lama

>   There is
>   kind thought
>   a way to be
>   an orchestra
>   with piano as one of the instruments
>   in imagination's role
>   touching on the last two centuries
>   but leaning toward
>   our own time as it indeed
>   changes – turns out
>   it was John Ireland's own
>   piano concerto
>   fresh splashes here and there.
>   The English know how to do everything
>   but talk well that's not fair
>   as the American right-wing drawl
>   is the worst-sounding thing on Earth
>   as the human non-family forgets
>   it's destroying its host, the Mother
>   the rich pollute and the poor, drained,
>   have nothing left but growing families
>   distraught by stress.
>   Not much hope there but in some
>   tiny world somewhere nothing is permanent
>   which is the record accomplishment
>   of Nature – hey Earthlings you're just
>   like everything else changing into more
>   change, after all, so many new stars are forming
> each day and through each of our little petty nights
> there is bound to be more of our happy family
> of self-worshiping species
> everywhere scattered throughout the universe
> evolving into greedy non-thinking minds
> well - kind thought - where are you hmmm
> I'm not dead yet but so many are
> where does all the culture go when we all go?
> on some miraculous golden disk flying
>   aimlessly through the cosmos?

    Breathe well and try to free a religious nut
    from a prison of cult conformity
or, like me, realize I ain't got any
solutions – maybe a greeting here and there
asking how *you* are, and a smile and eyes
that meet yours.

READING THOMAS MERTON IN THE BATHROOM

    His God does down the toilet
    but his words stay in my lap.

CELEBRITY TESTES

Time testes time testes
you want the other testes to be
testicular toast!
YOU are the only Testes except
the toad testes the little toady testes
we're all the testicular cult
with me the High Testes leader
of my titillating little toady testes.

THE MOVEMENT

    I will perform the first movement of
    the Movement to End All Movements.
    There will be no second movement.
    Uh-Oh I forgot!
    I've already performed it.

END OF DISCUSSION

People don't want to come over and talk
or rouse themselves in a good discussion.
They're afraid they might advertise themselves the wrong way
or present a distortion of who they are.
    Besides, it seems wrong to bust over into your home
    invading privacy, even when invited –
    smelling some odd odors or seeing
        a different arrangement of things.
Now it's okay to wail and rail at length
or epitomize the usual spurts of thinking
in a post which will elicit the familiar likes
hearts or careful stereotypical comments.

    People don't want to experience the exhaustion
    of having to think while actively taking into account
    the *actual presence of someone a yard or two away:*
    the hideaway post in bed under covers
        is much more convenient.
It's safer to go on that rail and wail
    of daily nightly all-time routine
and keep quiet about a lot of things –
especially career, standing, money, food
purchases and certainly
the horror of someone with a different opinion.

    People don't want to come over and talk
    or certainly not bother to call when
        you can sneak off a message
    certainly not leave an antiquated voice message.
    Face to face oblivion is much better
    as I opt back to familiarity, comfort,
    the mundane mundane of self-obsession.

Oh yeah, he did? He died? – I was just going to
    pick up the phone the other day
but didn't. He what, he did?
    He died of apprehension someone might see him alive?

THE HEALING

        Can things get better, plug in some
        cloud that has connection to
        the *there beyond* that has some grounding
        in cure, a benevolent cure or at least
        this power-that-be, connected to,
      wakes up to someone's particular need
     sickness malfunction mysterious
    and in most natural way, nature-bent and powerful
heals, brings to healing, solves the problem
of debilitating pain, the grace of lifting the useless
sickness, source demystified, and all
gets better is better is gifting to the sufferer
be in pain no more, the healing is set in
is working, the connections are made are heard
and resolved, the organic body heals
  walks freely, is as the grace of life is supposed to be.
  And yes. the letter to clouds worked!
    the faith in resolving connection to connection
      like powerful synapses, the brain and body of
      the universe – is listening.

INTO THE MYSTERY

Stare into substance and maybe you'll go to sleep –
stare in to the gloom of a foggy night
    the kind we don't have here.
Stare into the radio with the light off of course.
The classical sounds from some far off century –
let your mind travel to some distant planet
then snap back to your head on the pillow.
Soar off into a drippy nose with a
    handkerchief between your cheek and the pillow.
Get up for some water and the bathroom,
    again avoiding dark objects.
That's right – you'll never fall asleep again
or will you or won't you or will you.
Stare into the mystery of losing waking consciousness.

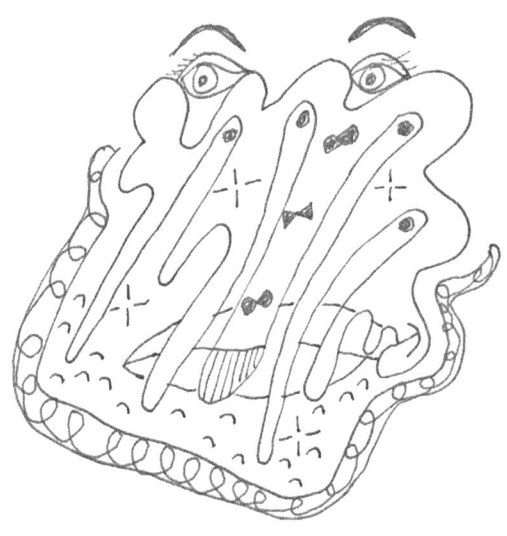

1ST OF MAY

I pray for a better day
sink my talons in the rich
and celebrate festivities.

WHY SHE KEEPS HER DISTANCE FROM AN OLIGARCH

He makes
so much money
he doesn't have to pee – all
body emissions are magically
laser spewn from the body in
microscopic perfumed darts
as his sperm cells molecularly
deposit themselves in any
fertile female's fallopian
tubes within 20 foot
distance
from
the
Billion
aire.

HEART

My heart is a choir that sings
"Never lose it, what you have attained
Don't let the limited dicks and the God-Awfuls
change your course –
for you it has been solitary surprise
traveling through the membranes of creativity and loosening up
for the voices at the edge of your universe
where ancient portals met the pettiness of what you were given
and revealed the actual heritage of true self.
*An amazing vocal and compassionate father
and a mother everybody loved."*

ADVICE TO MYSELF WHEN I GET BIGHEADED

"All you can generate is a low hum that is slightly below the range of hearing, or a high squeal that, again, nobody can hear. Your imprint on the world is water when you thought it was lust. All your vocal high energies played out before you made them. The turning point in your life was an everyday ho-hum, or was it hum drum. You recognize too late you were born yesterday. The friends you had are so sad that you remember them. Other than that your star got renamed by somebody else. What is that you said? Remember, the mirror has deaf ears. If you think you're a non-entity, think again: that word is too big. If there's going to be another chapter in your book it's got to follow the one you never wrote. Of course you can always gather your family around you but if you're already expired, *why bother?*"

SCREAMS: WEST 4^(TH) STREET, ACROSS FROM THE SPRING RIVER GOLF COURSE – HOMETOWN – EARLY 50'S

What I'm about to tell you
is a dialogue between two people
when one screams and yells
and the other doesn't listen.
One goes across from his house to
the edge of the golf course at night
and carries on shuddering and
crying sobbing trying to recover
then shouting to God over and over
why am I who I am, why am I
just suffering and hardly anything else?
The dark skies' impotence is
staggering, the stars heavy in that small
town are bright and indifferent.
Going back to bed, why dream, why do
anything different but the same thing over
and over. There are many places you
can go to scream and you can scream
without being heard. There is the
deafening silence of not listening which
is the nature of God, God in a medium
sized small town with a lot more Protestant
churches than Catholic, one small synagogue.
Are all their gods the same, buckled up
in their houses of worship
handing out sermons and hymns
and not hearing the screams that someone
like myself bullet out?
It is a world of a bulwark of silence that
your screams crackle against. And there's
the lonely separateness that your identity
presents to itself. You are one measure
alone in the quantity of your existence.

A CONCEPT OF THE PURE – ROSWELL ON

The covers are over your head. You don't want the world to find you. Where are you? I'm on Fifth Street in Roswell, New Mexico. It is becoming clear that something is becoming clear. There's a massive rock 10 feet high. Next to it is a fluff of cotton. I'm supposed to be the rock. I feel more like the cotton. Cotton in the fields where the black people pick and pick and slowly fill large canvas bags they drag behind them. And then their bag is tight-full and they're paid. All those fluffs of cotton with the hard seeds within. All smashed into the bag getting full and full as it can be, if it's a good worker. Packed with cotton as hard as a rock and you get paid at the scale. I tried it. I was absolutely no good. I picked and picked the white fluffs hard seeded and there was a small lump at the bottom of my big bag dragging behind me and when I was tired of the work I got paid a couple dollars.

That's what I usually thought about myself. Coming up short. Inadequate. That's what I drew for the psychiatrist years later when I saw him when I was called back into the Army and was supposed to report soon. I couldn't stand more Army. After all I just got out from two years of it and in the Mojave Desert.

And now because of Khrushchev and the Russians and Castro and the Cuban Missile Crisis I was supposed to go back into the Army to help out as Kennedy's show of muscle. When Dr. Roth asked me to draw myself I drew a rather weak person sitting in a chair. He said draw a man and it was a tall tough man. Draw a woman? A rather pretty woman sitting. And me there sitting hopeless. "You feel inadequate?" That was the word he used and that's what he wrote me as suffering from- "anxiety reaction." Dr. Roth wrote his statement I was unsuited for redeployment and put it in a small envelope that was sealed with adhesive tape. It worked. I was discharged right when the soldiers were all leaving for field duty at Fort Polk, Louisiana. I was out with a whole year's plans messed up.

SPRING SENTIMENT
/for Lenore

Truly in our 80's we are – we do feel enlightened by our love years 55 - truly 55 marriage sings through. Gardens of real work rototilling the nutrients in, you're down on knees preparing bed for each plant or the carefully planting those lettuce cabbage broccoli, setting in the tomatoes already started, jalapeños, some corn, eggplant and largely, bell peppers. Oh for the jalapeño bell pepper salsa to come!

It all goes by, your years of such full garden and the water of the Spirits of the Mountain, mountain-side home itself here almost 50 years. Time traces our origin back to student arts in Albuquerque, city on the breadth of Route 66, New York New Mexico, the making with hands and extraordinary minds of the utmost creative bold.

What you terminated in schooling was my beginning of life post-academic into evolving adventures – Mexico's Coatlicue and Monte Albán and here, perched up a bit higher than the Village, care taking and living – what food, what trips to the bar, what parties, what studies back into pre-Columbian trails, and giving birth – procedures difficult, separate and together.

We were SO happy to move into a new adobe, a house like us to grow. Now, having worked on this place, the water decreasing in climate desperation, focuses us on keeping fruit trees alive as you move your focus to all the surrounding native plants, photographing, identifying following the flowering, the changing year after year, some of the same places or to Petroglyphs, Open Space, Caldera on and on.

Nature continues evolving our lives our family struggles *unending*, and yet creating out to the indifferent world or into ourselves, our love and friends – but mostly you and I and ours.

The precise eye, the perfect eyes you have that bring discrimination to a new level. For me, often, the exact word, but for you always the exact sight, the precision of quality remains in all love, real love, ours and the best. As close as I think I know it can be, and is.

GROUND LIVING

You are the lifeline of my conscious corona
the harbinger of my herald of my past
    which has become my future.
Thank you for refusing to be the
    mirror of the beast
but the actuality of a beautiful flower
    full, white, a hint of fragrance
passing into now.
Simplicity reigns in the field Nature planted
    although the cosmic complication of its roots
        are the grounding of us all.

MARCH OF THE EMBRYOS

Now that Alabama has officially Christened embryos as children they are waking up to this new status and thawing themselves out and escaping the labs and even becoming unruly children! This has been happening in cryogenic labs across the country. Some embryos who escaped are ganging together and acting like kids in *Lord of the Fly*, taking over houses and causing havoc in neighborhoods. The embryos are small but when they band together they can do all kinds of things, like taking over trucks and sports cars and driving like maniacs on the highway and across people's lawns, and even causing adults to flee their houses.

Some embryos have taken over police departments managing to acquire little tiny police outfits. Others have invaded fundamentalist Christian churches demanding reparations and support: "You created our status so you've gotta support us! Here we are, give us money and shelter so we can grow and grow and become idiots like you!" The embryos are everywhere. They've escaped by the millions and we adults can't do anything about it because we all have equal status now. They're even getting on school boards and running for office and threatening to vote for the stupidest embryo of all.

JUST SAY HELLO

Love bites the tongue off complaints
there's a repartee
with hope around the corner
and you don't even have to dance!

FAWN FAWN

Fawn fawn the rabbit
evil cheese the chose
come back to me Brother
I never had to lose.

Longing is the last
and the first to come.
Fawn fawn the Brother
never last to choose.

SOME SAND PHOTOGRAPHS
/for Lenore

The exact nature of things as they are
the sands of time, the sands of nature
      but the distinct reality
as it is as it shall be in these photographs
like monuments to clear sight
the intense being of nature and sun caught
the gift of discernment and discovery
      precise clear focus
unquestionably real out of the sand into true light.

OLD WHITE DUDE
/put on old man mask
It's about time good guys
fellows gents chaps hombres buddies
stand up to the right-wing extremist fetishists,
the diehard pillow-faced, tight-assed, treacherous
bone-spurry cult buggers,
the sycophantic lying bullies
whose name "blisters our tongues"
Shakespeare had that phrase for Macbeth.

They have stenchified and rotted out airwaves
cable cell and digital signals suck assed into palaver –
RepubliCONS and other bonehead hypocrite noisomes
 back-ass their punitive poison into KKK fru fru
    screwy-laden falsehoods
      and wildly lying bullshitapoopoo
        their version of
           balls-hanging-from-their-noses "masculinity"
             trying to be as toxic as a supernova fart
               but not even coming up to
        a mosquito fart,
        a pinprick fart
        an electron fart
        a fartless
        fart.

Goodbye ugly spineless buffoons.
              /take off mask.

NATURE OF FEELINGS

I wish the human being could feel the passages of Earth in him
    in her intimately.
        And wish is a weak word. I *want,* I can't *will,* but I know
the Sandias, Turtle Mountain, in the last lingering sunlight
    the holder of snow, the fulfilling winter covering that gives us
this liberal water in its melt through mysterious underground linkings
    to our Springs here, old as old Village –

its rural history, its acequias, its acequia Madre
and winding ditches maintained by hand, down to our trees
our lessening gardens, our washing machines
and our bodies,
this dependence is interrelated, inter-felt.

And a caution to draw back the manipulation
the constantly demanding manipulating, extracting, killing
to control and benefit,
piercing constantly more wells without feeling the passages
of Earth planet changes, local changes,
Earth not increasing in size
only the proliferating humans increasing, the men and women
not feeling chemical and oil they persist in spewing out
from the planet engulfed in
foreign trapped gasses –
everything foreign is local, as the warming continues.

The Sandias, Mount Taylor, Sangre de Cristo,
Taos Mountains, Sierra Blanca, Jemez Mountains, and farther,
Sacramento and Organ Mountains, in *all*
we can feel their passages as humans proliferate and tycoons of the
worst sort
lose all humility and feeling and strive through force and ingeniously
concocted weapons elsewhere, even here,
to amass more to themselves, poisoning tragically more of the Planet.

There is no feeling left in these men for the Planet they depend on.
May all the mountains bring us back –
maybe pollinators *shouldn't* be destroyed, small farming *forced*
to dry up.
The human being can feel the passages of Earth rebelling
from the species' population injury
from the loss of the Spirit of the Breath in every animal and plant,
the feeling of *Earth Change*.
Giving birth again to cooperation and humility
awareness all these mountains are telling us, all beings natural
as we can be again, it is telling *saying*.

DEVELOPIT!

Develop the sky out of the sky.
Develop your *heart.* Can you take your heart to the bank?
How about an electronic transfer to your mutual fund
    and your stocks –
send your heart out. They'll bank on it.
Any bodily tissue you have, some business somewhere
can use it, transform it, make the investment
    everyone seeks, at least your friends or
should I be accurate, your acquaintances.

You have no friends unless you call someone
who'd just as soon knife your back a friend.
I mean you're in it for what you own in it, for you *own*
your breath, for instance, so isn't there a way
    to extract that *oxygen* and make money off it?
Your organs might bring you some bucks
but mostly keep your body intact and keep your
brain working for you. You've made it so far,
stormed into your small sleepy community
and woke it up – you and your friends – I mean
your acquaintances. Develop the hell out of
    every inch of property you can, erect
some *stick* homes quickly and smear on fake adobe
and advertise "Authentic Southwest Paradise."

A LOT TO TELL YOUR MOTHER

"Neurological potatoes"
    where the sky is full of fear.
There's a lot to tell your mother –
    things are not what they appear.

29 YEARS

What does it mean to be 29 years sober?
    Would I be dead if I blew the head off my beer
        for the many thousandth time
    and drank the cans dry and the bottles afterward?
        And gave my Christian soul to the inebriates?
That is, my Pagan soul, that is, my lack of soul.
Where would I be but a Zero, thinking back on
    years I lived?
I was a nonentity at year Zero when
I filled my flesh with nothing!
And I will be a Zero again if year 30 doesn't
    come around sober
        and I revert to a baby alcoholic!
Crying all the time why did I start again.

DID YOU DILLY DO?

Did you dilly do die and blue?
Were you married to a fool?
We tongue fed our twisters.
How far are we going,
    to the ends of the Earth?
All the way, someday.
At the Universe's speed where are you?
If you look through the window frame
    will you find tomorrow?

HELP TIME

Help with the circulation of the poles down to Earth.
In the fire. Keeping warm. Or illuminating a room.
What is the connection of the Sun to my heart?
The bud of the Buddhist. The seed of the Christian.
The dance of the Mohawk.
The touching the Earth with the beat of the drum.
Touching the drum with the beat of the Earth.
Concentration. Singleness. Momentary peace.

>   The gift of Mozart going down the drain, possibly,
>   from toxic testicles, men urging Earth destruction
>   through greed, in love with oil, annihilation
>   of culture for petty power –
>   loving arms turned into weapons.
>   Big business of big business, monopolistic price hikes.

Beware the world where the indigenous mother
has no hair on her son's head to braid.
The very young dancer is refused the sound of the drum
in the park, but he still dances. You know what that is?
Spiritual. Meaning. Breath. Meaning.
Intake. Out take. Meaning, hold it. Meaning, let it go.

>   I regret the loss of de Kooning if it comes to that,
>   or the sitting posture of Gertrude Stein, or rather,
>   let the feminine out. She dances in full regalia.
>   Incredibly beautiful – women in full Earth presence.
>   She is the beautiful plot of the story, newly discovered
>   right next to the TV. Her patience when everything is lost.
>   The end point is the vacuum of space where we reside
>   in gravitational movement, miraculously.
>   Questioning, an agonizing knot: has it all come to this
>   at the pit of my stomach? The powerful versus the simple.

The decision to not ride the wild bronco today.
The bucking of human beings terrorizing animals and plants
and other humans. Things are too tenuous to take any chances.
Petty destruction. Massive suffering. The virgin Planet
throwing off all her veils. Forced to dance destruction
    rather than creation? No.
When you find some way to light the candle the Sun hears.
Your prehistory hears. The matchless one time
in this part of the universe gift based on millennia
of evolved fruition responds.

> *You* are not crushing hope on the planet.
> The soft tissue is a fragrant flower. Spring. The Winter,
> love in the fear. Light the seed in darkness.
> The struggle of pain and sickness and aging and reckless,
> powerful forces beyond control, paused.
> Have the breath release in this narrow light.
> This special warmth that is the power that created
> the Universe. Accumulated in millennia this womb planet.
> To be cared for in simplicity. In blessing. In interpersonal
> communication. In Song. Words. Dance.

NO JOKE

        Loyalists of old
      pretending to be new,
    celebrity worshipers in
    a Celebrity Culture
 yearning and willing to fight for
the Grand Old Monarchy:

       "To hell with Paul Revere
       to hell with Tom Paine
       to hell with the Founding Fathers
       to hell with the Constitution
       to hell with Separation
       of Church and State.
       To hell with free speech
       and peaceful protest!

     "We want a King to lie to us
    and make us think we're fine
   and we can bathe ourselves in
    His glory again (and bring back rhyme).
  Worship His beautifully adorned
   F A M I L Y
 and their Palaces and
 look at the Jewels all
that gold and shining SPLENDORK!

"Oh to kiss the hem of HIM again
and scream
in crowds
of total submission.
God save the King!
Dick Tater Supreme!

      "To hell with equality
       to hell with freedom of speech
     to hell with separation
     of church and state,
   a joke!
  Orange Pig a Foofoo Forever!"

HEART BEAT

     My heart beats on what cue – does it follow some drum beat
something I can't hear but is its pattern cut out on paper maybe
    following along like a sewing machine in out in out
in out threading the lines hearing and responding tirelessly?
     I know there is a pattern somewhere falling down into my life
and I address it as my heart beats and I ask it who you are
    but the morning opens up better when I give up demanding
an answer – turmoil and sweat and shouting and crying
      comes to nothing - as my heart hears and continues to beat.

DEAD BEAT

    I get up to the sound of my true self
but I don't necessarily obey.
I'm not a follower but a detractor
and there is a price to pay.

The malaise can take over when
I thought I deserved a rest.
That mellows out into nothing
    happy to extend itself.

REFRESHING WORK

What happened to refreshing work
    turning over my mind
to uncover what was there before
    in my small world?
It veered off, I pushed it too
    just to complicate the day.
It leaves me with the sadness only
    I took it away.

BA BA

      It's time to die
       like an old piece of bacon
      burnt to a crisp
     a horse taking a drink from the tank
     and stumbling over a cliff
    a raccoon stealing dog food on the porch
    then shot by the owner
   like a spider someone intentionally
  steps on
or a mouse bang! caught in a trap breathing
a last breath
like a runner on his last run
the heart gives out
dead, searched for and found
cremated and remembered
just someone, anyone, suddenly
he is no more, she is no more
she's gone, they're gone, you want to die
and leave the terrifying axe of a lunatic
ego monster enjoying cutting off your head
 so he can feel bigger better more
  in control as he
   hoists his diapers over his head
    and pees on an anthill
     and farts sword farts.

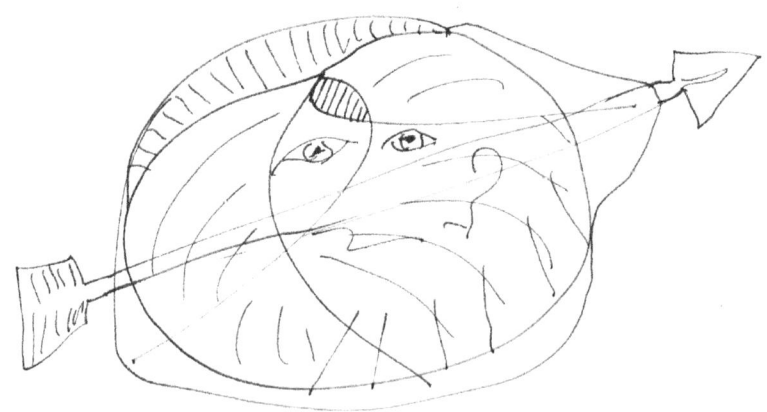

HOMAGE TO RENE CHAR AND HENRI MICHAUX

              Correct the Dharma and float toward God.
            Glue Jesus to Buddha in your craft class.
          Be humble that is, don't puke in the Bowery.
        Knit things together whether they can be knitted or not.
    Be a pickle therefore there is nothing you can do
       about yourself.
  You are your own imagination and not real.
Don't believe any of these voices.
Get up. Say your usual prayers. Make up
     a prayer that is honest.
You need to not give in to false articulation.
Everything comes down to walking carefully
     when you walk.
  Don't bang on things it leaves bruise
        splotches when you are old.
          Those great French poets had a handle on
             the absurdity of things
                which means you need a small group of
                    friends to set you right
                        and an honest shot of sunlight in the morning
                            and someone to love simply as the light.

CRASH BURN – *GIVE US SINGING!*

1.
As we crash burn falling into the chaos of
    religious impudence
we can remember who we are who we have been
born of this continent, primarily, even this state
this state of Union or coming to it from anywhere
trying to find some sense of life – here it is
never conquered and truly surviving born again
in the Womb of Mother Earth Father Son
I don't need a Middle East God that is
    so far away he could never touch
        the Earth here
He He He – Hehaw –   *Give us singing!*

2.
Here are the Four Corners, here are the Waters
the Sun Power and Earth present –
the great grandparents of the ancient peoples
already here, whose spirit is spirited
spirituAL – oldest stories of this homeland
can openly gift us with the simplicity of knowing
you don't need foreign gods, you need spiritual
    backers whose humility can only teach
unruly self-obsessed humans
how not to kill each other but to
    respect and nurture all the plants and
        animals that are just as much
            part of this earth as we are –
love, neighbors – plants and animal life are neighbors
as well as we humans who work together
        in the commons
the commons, working together to do and build things
    we all need
that is our blessing as we learn from the
original inhabitants of our own places here
      how to respect and work with and love
         where we are where we share. *Give us singing!*

3.
Forgive me for using we.
    I speak for myself.
I don't need any religious doctrine
shoved down my throat.
I live and breathe freedom to think for myself.
Men with rigid bipolar masculinity
are the dust of the past.
Women who have connections as natural as
    air and water and earth and art
are the foundation of a new era which is the oldest era
of fostering creativity family "hunting gathering farming"
    to a respected degree
nurture planet before personal wealth stars
and moon and clear sky and water earth stories
this planet is our master, our mother our solution
    to dissolving our bollocks ego
        into the paths of humility and
            commons building.
                Hear it
                heaving it
                the paths the Sun and Moon and Earth
                and ancient songs.

    Give us singin'!

AT TINGLEY BEACH PRESERVE
(on the wet path, cottonwood leaves covering)

    A moment's unveiling, revealing
     something I'm looking at
      emerges from surroundings.
       As every short once in awhile
      you suddenly dip into it
       from your staticky reality,
        the gift to humans,
         even with their vile content,
         revealed.
        But this rare condition,
       illumination of the greater real
       under the surface surfacing
      right where you look
     - you wish wasn't so rare -
    must continue to be itself -
    the impermanence of permanence.

TASKING

    What centers the soul in an achievable goal?
      The limitations of space – healing
          where you are or rather
       where I am
         only inhabiting *fully*
          the heartbeat, the *feet*
           the weight of your body on them
            on the ground
           the air, the light, the hearing
            the agony of the problems of others suddenly *released* –
         the narrowness of enjoyment, unpestered
       going into that space
           enjoying it as your mind leads you to do
     the routine, the complicated,
the task.

RAIN BARREL

Give me the roller coaster of peace
rather than the jackhammer of dissension –
the dimensions of regular living reach far and wide
up up ups and downs, deep downs
in just the hang it on, bumping on the ground living
but when disarranged thinking in someone dear
shatters the mood-swing-ordinary of daily living
you know your stress level will be shot to hell.

What can you do, you say, what to say when
the disarranged pain hits you from someone you love
or want to love or trying to understand
when even listening sometimes is forbidden –
someone is closed off.

I return to myself feeling useless until I face
and again enjoy the crazy ride of doing my dailies,
my ordinaries in the stash of creation, the uncertainty
and then release of being with someone I love and
am on the beam with and I can, say, get some water
from the rain barrels to a couple needy cherry trees,
walk into an imaginary circle on the ground
from the East
and pray loving healing to the few loved ones East
and again turning South, and again bring healing
West of course and North may the good come
East again then up, far up in universe reach and
down, this ground and below into the heated deep regions
and, centered, I can walk out the imaginary East door
and back to check on the water left in the rain barrel.

PORTRAIT OF DEFEAT

Portrait of a man with his skies on backwards
a lurid stare in the eyes that weren't his, but his father's.
Deception rules every block in his body.
There's a disconnect somewhere or is it everywhere?
His talent is to drive forth the crowds of his face
to drum his fingers on people's scrotums and
    napes of necks
as he entertains, as he asserts his power –
the "power" of weakness which is the worst power of all –
daring to say any goof brain thing that eggs him on.
His vat of sadistic sadness making them laugh
no matter what, built on Celebrity Status.
Everything is the Stage of Celebrity, the bric-a-brac
    of tinsel
coated with gold, dust of mines never found
as Nature runs backwards through his veins.

The hideous reign of others' terror is his laughing matter
tongues covering his neck, tongues entering his ears
    to his shrunken brain, tongues attached to every
crevice of his body, suited up for the next taunting oddity
audacity of cruelty with joked applause or rather claws
out for the land grab or rather gold coated heist
paced to kill for self and rupture of the spirit of others
pacing forward in backward's face.

How can any portrait reveal what's underneath,
    the atom eating molecules, hopelessly smashed
        and errant
making up the fatally concocted evolution gone wrong
    in a stub of thing in a stinging note of puce.

COOL JAZZ

Honesty regulates the fire that will burn up the world –
the more dishonesty the hotter the fire and nearer!
Only cool jazz will put it out in time
and the more cool jazz is outmoded
the hotter the fire gets as a volcano erupting
    with all the lies
adds to the heat pollution and the oven era
lights up the dawn as some cool jazz lover
in his small room plays Bill Evans Miles and Chet Baker
as the heat ascends spreads and bakes what was culture to a crisp
except one small concave of cool jazz
where Stan Getz plays on
and the sounds of Ella singing linger on as she
finishes her song.

LOOK!

    He brought the sunshine in
    and displayed it in
    buckets.

LOOKING AT THE PRESENT

Survival through shattering grace.

DICE YOUR POETRY

        Dice hard your poetry
        and add it to your dish
        some will find it too sweet
        but most will avoid it.

If you slice it
that will be nice
thin slices are best
for your perfect guest
but remember
you might just end up
eating it yourself.

        Sear your poetry
        in a medium hot pan
        add all the spices you want
        plus vegetables.
        Sounds like a hearty dish
        too bad you forgot
        to invite someone over.

But don't despair
someday somewhere
someone in the thin air
following your recipe
will half heartedly prepare
your dish
and be surprised
how much they enjoyed
your diced, sliced, seared
poetry faire.

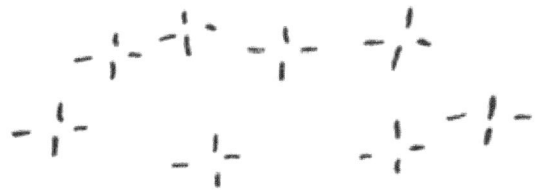

MAN MAIN MOAN

Please allow the intervention of Snakes
the taking over of Elephant mentality
the grasp of Ape thought
the alacrity of Crows
the dedication and clean up of Ants
the beauty and craft of Spiders
the prowess of the Lioness
the overwhelming diversity of thought of Wildlife
the explosive renewing of Nature
when Nature with a capital N
is allowed to take over
men man moan (the minus factor
of Planet Earth) – please allow
the immensity of the Jungle's reach
Trees buzzing with life dropping Seeds
as new growth can even reach a new Canopy
and the carbon dioxide captured into Renewing
instead of
enveloping and causing everything
to burn into a competing crisp.

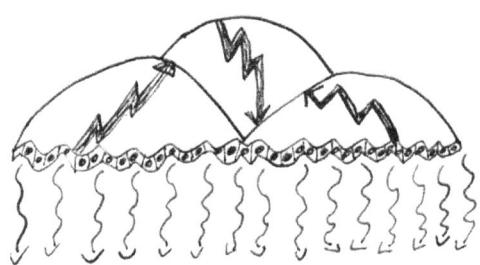

Out of crevice of granite grows
a desert marigold.

MADE FOR TV

Wake up Royal Goosehead!
The ants are crawling up your spine,
the honey bees have decided who to swarm on
    and sting.
Your upset stomach is suddenly drowning in
    Pepto Bismol.
The massage therapists in a ring around you
    have tried everything including
pommeling the inflated body with manicurists'
    long fingernails.
The Doctors and Omni-Specialists have tried
    brain transplants
    heart lung liver knee hip soul removal and
endless replacement body parts
as the Hired Priests and Loyalist Preachers
pray endlessly over the twitching, anticipatory body –
psychologists, brain listening shouting praise,
    extolling endlessly and giving up.
Still the living corpse of the world's most lying Zombie
continues to twitch and exude lie after lie even in
    its sleep
as green bubbling stench
exudes from all portions crevices and pores of
    the quasi-royal body.
The Bully Despot Supreme twitches, the effusive
    wannabee king
        spasms and vibrates
        exploding out a new chain of
        vociferous
        lies upon waking!
        Distortions
        pussy
        profusions
as his pretend magnificence jerks up suddenly
shouting into the row of
ogling lens of cameras nonstop,
ignorant slushes and sluices
abominations supreme.

SPRING WATER

I'm too worried to live sometimes I'm thinking. Thinking takes over my mind. Wish I could rinse it with the clothes. Don't need to wash, just fresh water. Sometimes I think that is the purest thing in our lives. Our water. Melts. And trickles down and sometimes flows. If there is the snow. Never thought there would be lack of water when we moved in. And no well. From all the crap in the atmosphere and planet warming. So here we are. Tragedies unravel. Regroup, get stronger.

People's lives at the will of their so-called leaders, well, they are leaders. To destruction. Masculine competition for the high chair. Wish it was the electric chair. They are babies. Without compassion there is no adulthood. And celebrities take over and run their mouths into our minds. And put down everything to build themselves up to be leaders with baby brains.

Back to water. What will we do if there isn't enough snow and rain? Will the National Guard bring trucks of water for us? Of course we can't have gardens, grow our own vegetables. Except a very small quantity, from saved water mostly. I will drink it with the appreciation. As long as we have it.

It doesn't help, the myriads of big new houses. All sucking the water out, as they overuse it. But then, as my Aunt once said, "Well, it's progress." She taught her children to be just as Republican as she. The only progress there can be is regress. Of the number of human beings. And how can that happen without massive cruelty? Who knows? I'm tired of the human race pestering Mother Earth. And not caring to care. This water is so precious. So delicious. So saving. Of grace.

ON THE RISE

    Right now a lot of people
        are gagging politely
on life –
the devil in his king shoes
is wiping his own country from
        the fat face of the Earth
and of course he will succeed –
kings and wannabe kings often do.

But what we vomit up won't
        be palatable to a
            king and his
                brown nose
                    court.
There just may come a nationwide gag fest
        a powerful heave into the
            golden toilet.
The crack of Congress is growing
and the parental Court system
stands on the Law in slow steps toward
        reversal.

As the lawless bite their lips
        and manoeuver even more
            to take over
you and me and some of them,
        almost all of us
        stand our guard
and shame the ass-kissers into
        partial action.

Every bit counts when it is
        a Constituent Rising
with everyone having a bone
        to pick with
stupidity and no-shows.

Time for everyone to show up
    gouging every corporate crack
with the Power of the People needling
    through.

A crack can become an Earthquake
    with Mother Earth an ally,
with the Constitution of We the People
    our voice.

Let Freedom ring in Democracy
    throughout
If more people show up
    and vote
their ghost is toast,
    their kingly puffery
    a joke -
more of us voting
    booming in size
always on the rise.

FOOTPRINTS

Following an unknown footprint
    is it barefoot or shoe?
It seems neither, a jump
    to the next one, very slowly
then quickly the next one, then
    I'm not certain, it seems lost
or could it have ended here,
    here where I am?

GOLDEN OPPORTUNITY

        The Super Rich everywhere
      are trying to be poor.
      They've been so despised
      they're craving humility.
     They're clambering!
    They're trying everything in the books
       to be poor!
   But they just don't know how to do it.
  Now what *you* could do is instruct them.
You could probably make quite a bit of money
    doing that
and doing that would help the poor Super Rich to be poor again.

The dawn eats dawn as the sunset dies, eaten alive.

TORN SHEET

    I could get up and march with the lizards
        to meet the dawn
    or luxuriate in clean sheets which RIP tear as I turn.
    The top of this old sheet with its zig-zag purpose
        quincunx and zig-zag lines in rows –
    tomorrow you'll be a useful rag, mini rags when torn up.
    Such bold acquisitions to live with all their lifelines
        thanks to the eye of Lenore –
    nothing could live in this house without her eyes' OK –
        but what doesn't have time limits?
    As I, old, have old possessions –
    Only Nature, in the real world out there
        when given free reign,
    proliferates and renews.

MORNING GLORY

Nothing stares me in the face. Maybe it's good to be blank.
Whatever happened to the *tabula rasa* – bring it back!
I have no heritage, no connection with anything.
They're all out there doing *their* thing.

I'm Mr. Nothing and I'm proud of it – things are pretty low key here.
All the directions are out, out and away and I
can better stay in the vacuum I'm in.

True, I am rotating slowly around the sun
and my body is turning slowly, always to the left
and I'm slowly climbing, and as a matter of fact I'm always
seeking the sun, sunlight my direction for attention.
And in my own way I am strong but I don't live forever
I mean I don't I can't I simply am the genteel nothing –
I've always fought, sought, failed to reach some
hysterical pinnacle some broadcasting blabbermouth entity
like some loud speaker somewhere fed by a battery losing power
hear that squawk? That's *me* wanting to be seen and heard.

Well, you win. Take the pennant and run with it –
it's all yours. I'll have my chicken pot pie and
some lettuce leaves and maybe a banana.
Got any plans? Don't include me – oh, that never crossed your mind.
This is the way I want it, I tell myself – look at the
gross artless panorama out there – the stupid *foundation*
and all the misery built on it, yes, everything everywhere so busy.
Fine distinctions and enjoyable quality of things is so good
but the harpies, arguing over and picking up the pieces,
while they build their egos up and crash burn each other –
power entities after power entities yelling out or
     pretending to be friends
as they *suck ass* and *knife backs* in the same gesture.

There's a plant here growing toward the sun –
Good luck! You will flower, I know
with no help from the busy body world.
Nor do I want that, as I look straight into the non, the nothing,
    the intense vast vacuum
        of space.
Spinning like the planet I'm on in a universe so enormous,
    so beyond comprehension
the absurdity of it – and me just being me, minutely so, is comforting.

/June 20, 2025
90th Birthday – read at home to friends

CODA

SPIRIT OR BREATH

"Thinking of the spirit of death. Oh, pardon me, thinking of the spirit or breath of someone. If they're dead, it's only the spirit combined in memory of them. But if they're living, I ask myself, "If they were dead what do I wish I'd asked them or talked to them about."

"Pretending that someone you know who is living, pretending that they are dead, allows me to know exactly how I will feel when they actually do die. The breath has gone out. Respiratory finish of how I can think about them, what I can think about them. The memory world, what is left. For living friends or acquaintances the spirit and the breath are both alive. Not just the Spirit which is alive only in memory. And I can ask myself what is the spirit of our friendship or acquaintanceship? Is it limited, falling short in true questions, questions that I can actually ask?

"I can resolve to broaden a living friendship successfully, until death. The combination of the breath and spirit of someone I know is a most living thing. And it sometimes aches to be expanded and fulfilled but gets put off till too late. A relationship may want to feel more embraced, conversed or loved.

"My life is full of spirits now. So many friends show me they could be dear friends if I broaden the breath which, in turn, informs the spirit. It recognizes its history, it's progenitor, it's parent to what's going on now. I treasure the spirits that are the nature of memories. And I will try to live in both breath and spirit of living friends and those who I'd like to get to know better. So that when only the Spirit is left I won't have that rather painful regret that I hadn't taken advantage of their living Breath, but instead, I have informed and fulfilled and broadened and clarified before the last breath."

love mends
love amends

clouds
END

clouds

poems 2020-2025

Contents I	Deep Prayer 20
1st of May 110	Developit! 122
29 Years 123	Diagnosis 91
85 + ... 87	Dice Your Poetry 137
A Concept of the Pure – Roswell 140	Did You Dilly Do? 123
A Lot to Tell Your Mother 122	Diversity Wins 15
Advice to Myself 112	Do-Nothings 2
After the Great Ball Bust 60	Dry Aphrodite 80
After the Last Game 42	Earth Gifts 52
Air 90	Earthquake 47
Along 30	Echo 31
And Then There's Putin 74	Einsteinian Romance 61
Are People People? 5	The Elements of Love 66
Are You Prepared? 49	Empty for You 67
Are You? Are You? 21	End of Discussion 108
Arrest the Dawn 14	End of Times 33
At Tingley Beach Preserve 132	Equal Entry for All 18
Ba Ba 128	Equivalency 26
Back to Nature 57	"Even the Dogs" 96
Beautiful Nature 67	Evil 94
Blow out 8	Fawn Fawn 118
Blue Space 51	Fire Flood – Death of Oligarchs . 84
Book 101 Syllabus 4	The First Junco 55
Boy Toy 16	First Step 83
Brain Weather 64	Flyswatter 92
Care 88	Fool 68
Carrier 73	Footprints 142
Caught up 55	For Jess Harper & Slim Sherman 34
Celebrity Testes 107	For Joanie - Singer 45
Connect Me 33	For Lenore 102
Content 81	Free Free Free 0
Cool Jazz 136	Garden Retablo 6
Concept of the Pure 115	Generations 93
Courage at Naptime 38	Gloomy Gloom 105
Crash Burn – *Give Us Singing!* . . 130	Golden Opportunity 141
Crazy 14	The Greats: Ginsburg & Lewis . . 29
Creator 51	Ground Living 117
Crevice 17	Guns Galore 72
Dark Opera 76	"Have Mercy on My Soul" 80
Dawn Winter 13	The Healing 109
Dead Beat 127	Heard a Laugh? 35

Heart to Heart 73	Offhand Healing 86
Heart Beat 127	Old White Dude 119
Heart 112	On this Day November 16th 62
Help Time 124	On the Rise 142
High Meadow 85	One Single Man 11
Homage to Char and Michaux . . 129	The Pain 12
Hypocrite 32	Peter Karassik Laughing 36
I Don't like You 71	Plight 21
I'm the Me I Want to Be 104	Poet 9
Impossibility of Escape 95	Pointing it out 42
The Indefinite Definite 41	"Pootin" 72
Inevitability? 89	Portrait of the Mirror 76
Into the Mystery 110	Portrait of Defeat 135
Just Say Hello 118	Protectors 41
L!e!a!d!e!r 34	Purpose 10
Liar 32	Quiet Speeds the Light 30
Look! 136	Rad Way 92
Looking at the Present 136	Rain Barrel 134
Lovers 59	Rain Run Raw Water 78
Lullaby 49	Received 44
Made for TV 139	Refreshing Work 127
Man Main Moan 138	Relations 88
March of the Embryos 117	Retribution from Fire 90
Miming Sappho 43	Romancer 22
Mind Rot 81	Routine 43
Momentary Release into Now . . . 96	Sand Verbena near Ojito 27
Morning Glory 146	Screams: West 4th Street 114
More than Once the Stars 82	Screw Loose 1
Mother of God 79	Sentiments 40
Mother One 56	Serpent Meditation 97
Mousetrap - for Levi Romero 70	Seventies Brother 86
The Movement 107	Simple Life 7
Mowed down by Reality 28	Some Sand Photographs 118
Mutual 41	Song of Diversity 93
"My Religion Is Kindness" 106	Source 100
Native Spirit 12	The Space Between 48
Natives 13	Spirit or Breath 149
Nature of Feelings 120	Spirit Loss 64
New Mexico Song 82	Spittoonery 3
No Ropes Attached 65	Spring Sentiment 116
No Joke 126	Spring Water 141
Notes 39	Sun Moon 39
Nuts 24	Sunbathing 3
The Obvious 94	Super Modern Romance 61
Octavision 23	Supreme Court Prohibits Sperm 79

The Syringe Warts Have Come . .84	Uselessness 90
T-I-T-U-S 89	What If 2
Tasking 133	What Happened to the Sonnet. . 83
Teachers 69	What Can Be Saved? 25
Thinking Thou Art. 46	What I Did 11
Thunderbird Bar and Pool 45	What Eyes. 55
Timetable 66	White on Whites 35
To the Dawn - in Winter. 58	Why She Keeps Her Distance. . . 111
Tongues of Babylon 24	Winter Solstice – Placitas 98
Top of the Dung Heap. 39	With the Flow 54
Torn Sheet 145	Without Saying 51
Touching Spirit 27	Yes! 52
The Trumpeta Line!. 85	The You in You. 26
Trust Song 78	Zelenskyy and Compatriots 99

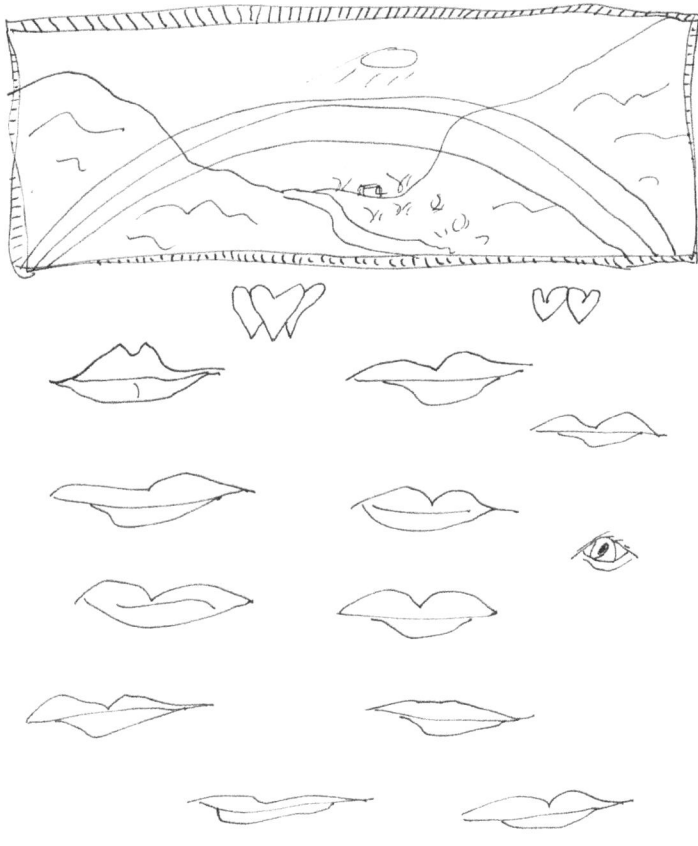

"Larry Goodell . . . one of the first poets to fully embrace Performance, from the 1960s onwards, incorporating hand-sewn costumes, props, his own piano playing, collaborating with musicians and dance troupes, etc."
John Roche

"Larry was a prime mover of Duende for decades, producing a fine series of events, many of which he recorded. This labor of love, along with years of similar work at Albuquerque's historic Living Batch Bookstore, constitutes an immensely rich archive of readings by generations of US American poets. Larry's contribution as self-proclaimed archivist is one of his many gifts to us. A powerful poet, having produced both books and productions that combine the spoken word with movement and visual art. His work – potent and satiric – is particularly important as a counterweight to today's climate of robot-like praise for neofascism and mediocrity."
Margaret Randall

BOOKSHELF DELIGHTS BY LARRY GOODELL

Drawings - drawings by Peter Karassik 104 pp.
A New Land and Other Writings - prose (New Edition), 168 pp. duende press 2024

Making it - 1968 poems and event performances, 137 pp.
Dance Book - collaborations with dancers, 97 pp.
Between Ann and Larry - Letters Ann Quin & Larry Goodell, 171 pp.
Breath - poems 2000-2002, 204 pp. duende press 2021

Escape - poems 2003 - 2007, 215 pp.
Grounded - poems 2008-2010, 229 pp.
Commons - poems 2017-2019, 240 pp. duende press 2020

Hot Art and Other Plays 2019, 222 pp.
Nothing To Laugh About - poems 2015-2016, 178 pp. Beatlick Press, Albuquerque 2018

Broken Garden - poems 2011-2012, 196 pp.
Digital Remains - poems 2013, 157 pp.
Pieces of Heart - poems 2014, 140 pp. Beatlick Press Albuquerque 2015
        Available from Amazon Books

ONLINE DELIGHTS

3 Dimensional Poetry   https://larrygoodell.blogspot.com/
Lotsa Larry Goodell   https://larrygoodell.wordpress.com/
duende.bandcamp.com music, poetry, plays

           DUENDE PRESS
           the original -   cover design Lenore Goodell
           larrynewmex@gmail.com   larrygoodell.com

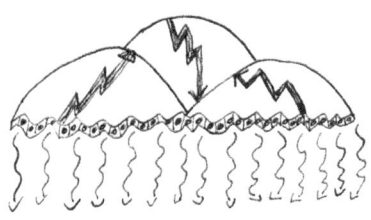

"The Larry Goodell / Duende Archive is a unique record of the thriving poetry and small press cultures of the Southwest (and New Mexico in particular) from the early 1960s to the present."
Granary Books / Larry Goodell / Beinecke Library
and for *sets of duende press* inquire
https://www.granarybooks.com/
or the author

Made in the USA
Monee, IL
19 August 2025

22588194R00100